T0270145

EVERYBODY LOVES
CHOCOLATE

Jennifer Donovan

EVERYBODY LOVES
CHOCOLATE

Delicious recipes from around the world

NOURISH

EAT WELL, LIVE WELL

Everybody Loves Chocolate

Jennifer Donovan

First published as The *Big Book of Chocolate*
in the UK and USA in 2008
by Duncan Baird Publishers Ltd

This edition published in the UK and USA
in 2024 by Nourish, an imprint of
Watkins Media Limited
Unit 11, Shepperton House
89-89 Shepperton Road
London N1 3DF

enquiries@nourishbooks.com

Copyright © Watkins Media Limited 2024
Text and recipes copyright © Jennifer Donovan 2008,
2024
Photography copyright © Shutterstock 2024
Photography copyright for pages 26, 38, 61, 65,
69, 73, 91, 117, 123, 124, 129, 139, 147, 153,
162, 130, 133, 136, 143 © Watkins Media Limited
2008, 2024

The right of Jennifer Donovan to be identified as the
Author of this text has been asserted in accordance
with the Copyright, Designs and Patents Act of 1988.

All rights reserved. No part of this book may be
reproduced in any form or by any electronic or
mechanical means, including information storage
and retrieval systems, without permission in writing
from the publisher, except by a reviewer who may
quote brief passages in a review.

Publisher: Watkins Publishing
Editor: Wendy Hobson, Lucy Carroll & Brittany
Willis
Cover Design: Lucy Sykes-Thompson
Head of Design: Karen Smith
Designer: Manisha Patel & Sneha Alexander
Production: Uzma Taj

For commissioned photography:
Commissioned photographer: Martin Poole
& Victoria Macken
Food Stylist: Aya Nishimura
Prop Stylist: Wei Tang

A CIP record for this book is available from
the British Library

ISBN: 978-1-78678-877-1 (Hardback)
ISBN: 978-1-78678-910-5 (ebook)

10 9 8 7 6 5 4 3 2 1

Printed in China

Publisher's note

While every care has been taken in compiling
the recipes for this book, Watkins Media Limited,
or any other persons who have been involved
in working on this publication, cannot accept
responsibility for any errors or omissions,
inadvertent or not, that may be found in the recipes
or text, nor for any problems that may arise as a
result of preparing one of these recipes. If you are
pregnant or breastfeeding or have any special
dietary requirements or medical conditions, it is
advisable to consult a medical professional before
following any of the recipes contained in this book.

Notes on the recipes

Unless otherwise stated:
- Use free-range eggs and poultry
- Use medium-size fruit and vegetables
- Use large eggs (UK) or extra large eggs (US)
- Use fresh ingredients, including herbs and chillies
- Do not mix metric and imperial measurements
- 1 tsp = 5ml 1 tbsp = 15ml 1 cup = 250ml

nourishbooks.com

CONTENTS

INTRODUCTION

There are few things in the world that evoke such intense emotions as chocolate. Silky, smooth and sensuous, chocolate has been around for centuries. It is thought to have been discovered in Mexico by the Aztecs, and then brought to Spain in the 16th century. It is believed that the Aztecs first used beans from the cacao tree to make a drink for royal occasions, and that the Spaniards made this bitter drink more palatable by adding cane sugar and spices such as cinnamon and vanilla. By the 17th century, drinking chocolate was considered fashionable throughout Europe, and by the 19th century, chocolate to eat had been developed, and traditional hand-manufacturing methods for making chocolates gave way to mass production.

Today, chocolate has become more popular than ever around the globe with gourmet chocolate boutiques catering for the growing passion for top-quality chocolate. Consumers are demanding better-sourced and higher-quality ingredients, so Fairtrade chocolate (where the cocoa beans have been sourced direct from farmers at prices that allow the farming communities to thrive and expand) and organic chocolate are both reaching a wider market.

This comprehensive book explains all you need to know about chocolate. It guides the home cook through a range of delicious chocolate recipes including fabulous homemade cakes, brownies, ice creams, desserts and muffins as well as spectacular desserts and handmade chocolates. Some of them will be familiar favourites, while others will provide some new and exciting ways to use chocolate with traditional recipes from other parts of the world.

Usefully arranged by location – The Americas; Asia Pacific; Europe; and the Middle East & Africa – the book showcases chocolate recipes from around the world. Some recipes are distinct to a specific country, for example Israeli White Chocolate Cheesecake (see page 168), while others share origins. Chocolate Lamingtons (see page 112), for example, are popular in both Australia and New Zealand with some debate about who created the original idea. Other recipes demonstrate a melding of cultures to create treats such as Matcha & White Chocolate Blondies (see page 84), while some deliver the flavour profile of a region, for example, the Middle Eastern flavours of sesame and honey in Chocolate Dipped Sesame & Honey Brittle (see page 170).

In addition to providing a wealth of simple-to-follow recipes, and briefly outlining the origins of chocolate, this book explains in simple terms the most common ingredients and methods used when cooking with chocolate – all designed to make the recipes even easier for you to reproduce at home.

WHAT IS CHOCOLATE?

Cocoa beans, from which chocolate is derived, are a product of the cacao tree. This is believed to have originated in the tropical areas of South America, although the exact location is a source of some dispute.

A relatively delicate plant, the cacao tree needs protection from wind and a good amount of shade; it usually bears fruit in the fifth year of cultivation in natural conditions. Although there are around 20 different varieties of cacao plant, only three are widely used in the making of chocolate – Forastero, Crillo and Trinitero.

The fruit of the cacao plant, known as "pods", contain between 20–50 cream-coloured beans, and it takes around 400 beans to make just 500g/1lb 2oz chocolate. The beans are fermented, dried, cleaned and roasted. Then the roasted beans are ground to produce a thick cacao liquor, or cacao mass, and finally pressed to extract the fat, known as cocoa butter.

Cacao liquor and cocoa butter are the essential ingredients of any chocolate product, and the amount included varies from around 25 per cent of the product's weight up to approximately 80 per cent, occasionally more. Other ingredients, including sugar, vanilla and milk, are added to the chocolate before it goes through the final processing stages. Generally, the sweeter the chocolate, the more sugar has been added and the less cacao liquor and cocoa butter it contains. The darker and more bitter the chocolate, the higher the cacao liquor and cocoa butter content; this is widely considered to be a superior chocolate. However, chocolate preferences vary between individuals, so it is best to experiment with what you have available to see which you prefer.

TYPES OF CHOCOLATE

There are a number of basic categories of chocolate. The first is dark (bittersweet) chocolate, sometimes referred to as plain chocolate or couverture. This is designed for both eating and cooking. Look for chocolate with a high cocoa content (usually marked as a percentage on the label). Ideally, the percentage should be somewhere between 70 and 85 per cent, although it is important to remember what you are ultimately using it for. The most readily available chocolate tends to range between 60 and 70 per cent, which renders good results, though higher percentages do exist.

The recipes in this book have all been made from dark chocolate (where specified) with a cocoa butter content of 70 per cent. However, if you want to enjoy the best-quality chocolate straight from the packet, be aware that many people prefer the highest cocoa solids content they can find, which can be up to about 85 per cent. I prefer not to use a chocolate of that percentage for cooking as the result can often be too bitter for a chocolate sauce or cake, which requires a slightly sweeter finish.

Also commonly available is milk chocolate, which generally contains less than 3 per cent cocoa solids, and has sugar, milk powder and vanilla added. Milk chocolate is not as successful in baking and cooking as dark chocolate, but you can happily use it as a substitute in mousses, fillings, drinks and cookies, particularly if they are destined for children, who prefer the less bitter flavour. However, once again, for the tastiest results look for good-quality milk chocolate, as many manufacturers use vegetable oils, artificial flavours, fillers and milk solids in their products. Organic varieties of chocolate make a good choice here.

White chocolate is another widely available product, although it is technically not chocolate at all. This is because white chocolate does not contain cacao liquor, instead being made from cocoa butter, sugar, milk and vanilla. Although not a pure chocolate, white chocolate is still very popular and gives good results in cooking.

Cocoa powder and drinking chocolate are also derived from chocolate. "Dutch-processed" cocoa, where the cocoa is treated with an alkali to give a slightly different flavour and a darker appearance, is considered to give the best taste. Cocoa powder is derived from the pressed cake that remains after

most of the cocoa butter has been removed. It may have 10 per cent or more cocoa butter content. Most commercial drinking chocolate (which is designed to be made into a hot or cold drink) is usually made from a mixture of cocoa powder and sugar. Both cocoa powder and drinking chocolate have their uses in cooking, but, as with chocolate, the quality does vary, so experiment with the different brands and buy the best you can afford.

STORING CHOCOLATE

As a rough guide, chocolate will keep for a year if stored in the correct conditions. Store in a cool place – around 20°C (70°F) – and don't refrigerate it unless the room temperature is very hot, as the moist environment of the refrigerator will shorten the life of the chocolate. Chocolate also absorbs the odours of foods stored around it, so be sure to keep it wrapped tightly in cling film (plastic wrap) or in a container with a tight-fitting lid.

The white film sometimes found on chocolate that has been stored incorrectly is called a "bloom". This is caused by condensation that has melted the surface sugar on the chocolate, and although it will not taste or look as nice as chocolate in good condition, it can still be used for melting or baking.

COOK'S INGREDIENTS

Most of the ingredients used for the recipes in this book are widely available and are often very standard, but it is worth noting a few specific points.

- **Butter** – all recipes, unless otherwise stated, use salted butter.
- **Eggs** – large eggs (extra large in the US) are used in all the recipes

Some recipes contain raw eggs, which carry a slight risk of salmonella, and should therefore be served with care and not be given to small children, pregnant women or the elderly.

- **Flour** – plain (all-purpose) flour and self-raising flour are used throughout this book. If you do not have any self-raising, and need to make some, simply add 1½ tsp baking powder and ½ tsp salt to every 125g/4½oz/1 cup plain flour.
- **Gold leaf** – this is an edible product and is most commonly available from specialist cake-decorating suppliers.
- **Leaf gelatine** – this comes in solid sheets that you soak in cold water until they soften. They dissolve easily in very warm liquid. Where necessary, you can substitute powdered gelatine – 10g/¼oz will set around 500ml/17fl oz/2 cups liquid.
- **Sugar** – caster sugar is used predominantly in the baking section of this book because its fine-grained quality gives the best results. (In the US, granulated sugar can be substituted in most of the recipes, except where superfine is stated.)

COOK'S TOOLS

You will not need much specialist equipment when working with chocolate. The recipes in this book use a standard range of kitchen utensils, including loose-bottomed spring-form cake pans and fluted tart pans in a variety of shapes and sizes. However, some items you may not already have do make the process that much easier.

- **Baking beans** (pie weights) – these are ceramic beads that are used to weight a pastry case when baked "blind", that is without a filling.
- **Baking paper** (sometimes called baking parchment) – this is used for lining tins and baking trays. It is better than greaseproof paper.
- **Double boiler** – this consists of a saucepan fitted with a smaller pan on top. The base pan holds water, which is heated, while the ingredients sit in the top, away from direct contact with the heat. It is useful for heating and melting delicate ingredients such as chocolate and egg custards. A heatproof bowl (such as glass or ceramic) set over a pan of simmering water will work too.
- **Electric hand mixer** – this will enable you to beat and whisk ingredients with the minimum of effort. Alternatively, use a hand whisk or free-standing electric mixer (where applicable).
- **Food processor** – use this to blitz biscuits (cookies) for crumb crusts and to bind cookie dough, among other culinary jobs.
- **Baking trays and tins** – use non-stick bakeware where possible, ideally silicone, which is durable and flexible. Note that cake and flan tins come in various depths, and it is important to use the recommended depth to avoid having too much or too little filling. Choose tins with loose bottoms for ease.

COOKING TECHNIQUES

Here are three main techniques we'll be using in our recipes:

1. **Using a bain-marie** – this French cookery term refers to a "water bath". You use this method to cook food in the oven very gently (often fragile dishes such as baked custards) and to prevent overcooking. You place the dish in which the food is cooked inside a larger vessel (sometimes with a cloth underneath to protect the base), which you then fill with water to come halfway up the dish.

2. **Melting chocolate** – chocolate is a delicate product and can burn easily. It melts best at temperatures between 40°C/104°F and 45°C/113°F. A double boiler is effective (see opposite), and prevents the chocolate from overheating, but you can also melt chocolate in a single saucepan directly on the stove over a very low heat, as long as you watch it closely and stir it gently. Alternatively, you can use a microwave oven. As the time needed will vary according to the amount of chocolate to be melted and the power of the oven, it's best to experiment to find out what works best for you. As a guide, use 30-second bursts until the chocolate has melted, stirring gently in between.

3. **Tempering** – this is a process involving the heating and cooling of chocolate at specific temperatures, which stabilizes the chocolate and gives it a shiny appearance. It also gives the chocolate a hard texture. Tempering is mainly used by professional chocolate makers, and can be done by hand or by machine. This process is not necessary for the recipes throughout this book.

FINISHING TOUCHES

Chocolate curls, leaves and piped shapes are simple to make and add a special touch to the final product. Here's how to make them:

- **Making chocolate curls** – a simple way is to sweep a wide-bladed vegetable peeler over a block of chocolate. Keep the chocolate cool, or the curls will lose their shape. A slightly more complicated way is to spread melted chocolate over a marble slab, if you have one, or the back of a large metal baking tray. Leave to cool, and then slide a long-bladed knife along the surface of the chocolate to create a curl. This can take a little practise, but is very rewarding. You can use this technique with dark, milk or white chocolate, or a combination of two or more, which can look quite impressive.

- **Making chocolate leaves** – simply brush melted chocolate on the back of a clean, well-defined leaf and chill. When cold, simply peel off the leaf, leaving a delicate imprint of veins on the chocolate.

- **Piping chocolate shapes and lines** – you can pipe chocolate shapes with a fine nozzle on to baking paper – but don't make them too delicate, or they will fall apart. Chill, then lift off as required. You can also randomly pipe lines of dark and white chocolate quite densely over baking paper, then set aside to chill, and break off pieces as required. This is a simple and effective method of decorating ice creams, mousses and meringues.

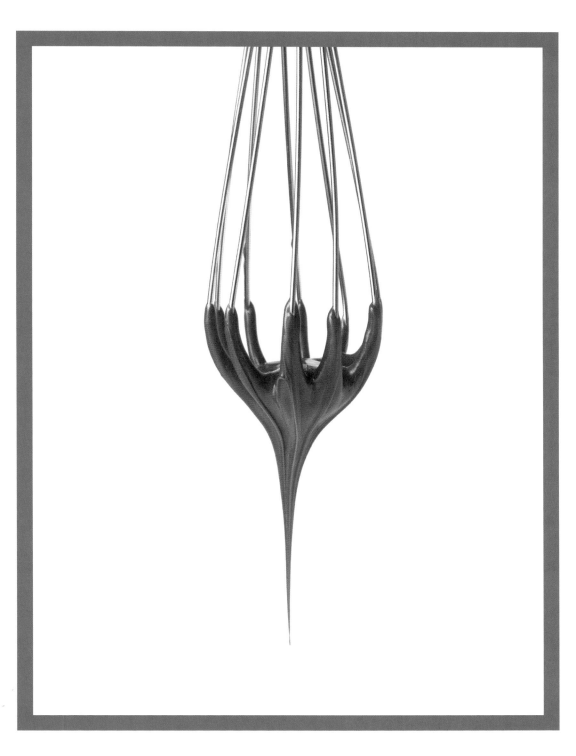

BASIC RECIPES

Chocolate Crumb Crust

PREPARATION TIME: 10 minutes
COOKING TIME: 10 minutes

MAKES: 1 x 23cm/
9in crumb crust

250g/9oz digestive
  biscuits (graham crackers)
2 tbsp unsweetened cocoa
  powder
75g/2¾oz/5 tbsp butter,
  melted

1 Preheat the oven to 200°C/400°F/gas 6.

2 Break up the biscuits roughly with your hands, then pulse them in a food processor (or place them in a plastic food bag and crush with a rolling pin) until they are fine crumbs. Add the cocoa powder and melted butter and pulse until the mixture is well combined.

3 Tip the mixture into a greased 23cm/9in spring-form cake pan, press it evenly over the base and up the sides of the pan (according to the recipe) and bake in the hot oven for 10 minutes. Remove from the oven and leave the crust to cool completely before removing it from the pan.

Chocolate Chantilly Cream

PREPARATION TIME: 15 minutes

MAKES: 250ml/
9fl oz/1 cup

250ml/9fl oz/1 cup
  double (heavy) cream
2 tbsp icing (confectioners')
  sugar
100g/3½oz dark
  (bittersweet) or milk
  chocolate, melted and
  left to cool

1 In a large bowl, whip the cream and icing sugar together to form soft peaks using an electric hand mixer.

2 Gently fold in the melted chocolate until just combined before using.

BASIC
RECIPES

Choux Pastry

PREPARATION TIME: 10 minutes
COOKING TIME: 5 minutes

MAKES: 6 large éclairs
or 12 profiteroles

2 tsp caster
   (granulated) sugar
60g/2¼oz/¼ cup chilled
   butter, chopped
90g/3¼oz/¾ cup plain
   (all-purpose) flour, sifted
2 eggs, lightly beaten

1 In a medium-size saucepan, combine the sugar, butter and 185ml/6fl oz/¾ cup water over a low heat and stir constantly until the butter has just melted. Remove from the heat and add the flour all at once to the butter mixture, stirring well with a wooden spoon. The mixture will form a thick dough.

2 Return the saucepan to the heat and continue stirring for 1 minute, or until the dough comes away from the sides of the saucepan.

3 Remove the saucepan from the heat and gradually beat in the eggs using an electric hand mixer. For best results, use the dough while still warm.

Sweet Shortcrust Pastry

PREPARATION TIME: 10 minutes, plus chilling
COOKING TIME: 30–35 minutes

MAKES: 1 x 23cm/9in pastry case or 4–6 individual pastry cases

250g/9oz/2 cups plain (all-purpose) flour, plus extra for rolling out
3 tbsp icing (confectioners') sugar
150g/5½oz/½ cup chilled butter, chopped
2 egg yolks

1 In a large bowl, combine the flour and icing sugar. Add the butter and rub it in with your fingertips until it forms small crumbs. (Alternatively, do this in a food processor, but work quickly or the pastry will be tough.) Work in the egg yolks and just enough of 2 tbsp iced water to form a dough using a flat-bladed knife or spatula. Note that the less water you use, the more tender the pastry will be. Wrap the dough in cling film (plastic wrap) and refrigerate for 15 minutes.

2 Preheat the oven to 180°C/350°F/gas 4. Roll out the pastry on a lightly floured surface to roughly 5mm/¼in thick to fit a 23cm/9in fluted loose-bottomed tart pan, 3–4cm/1¼– 1½in deep. Place the pastry in the pan to form a pastry case, taking care not to stretch it, and trim around the edge.

EVERYBODY LOVES CHOCOLATE

3 Line the pastry case with baking paper and fill with baking beans (pie weights). Cook in the hot oven for 20–25 minutes, then remove from the oven and gently lift out the paper and beans. Return the pan to the oven for a further 8–10 minutes, or until the pastry is dry and golden brown. (Alternatively, divide the pastry into 4 or 6 pieces and roll each one out to fit a 10cm/4in fluted loose-bottomed tart pan, 3–4cm/1¼–1½in deep. Line and fill as above and cook for 10–12 minutes, then lift out the paper and beans and cook for a further 5–7 minutes.)

VARIATION
To make Chocolate Shortcrust Pastry, add 1 tbsp unsweetened cocoa powder with the flour and cook the pastry until it is dry and dark brown.

BASIC RECIPES

Double Chocolate Sauce

PREPARATION TIME: 10 minutes
COOKING TIME: 5 minutes

MAKES: 250ml/
9fl oz/1 cup

125ml/4fl oz/½ cup
  double (heavy) cream
100g/3½oz dark
  (bittersweet) chocolate,
  broken into pieces
25g/1oz milk chocolate,
  broken into pieces

1 In a small saucepan, heat the cream until just boiling. Remove the pan from the heat.

2 Add both chocolates, stirring with a wooden spoon until they have melted, then serve warm.

Rich Chocolate Sauce

PREPARATION TIME: 10 minutes
COOKING TIME: 5 minutes

MAKES: 375ml/
13fl oz/ 1½ cups

250ml/9fl oz/1 cup
  double (heavy) cream
150g/5½oz dark
  (bittersweet) chocolate,
  broken into pieces
1 tbsp chocolate liqueur
  (optional)
1 tbsp icing (confectioners')
  sugar
1 tsp vanilla extract

1 In a small saucepan, combine the cream and chocolate over a low heat, stirring with a wooden spoon until smooth. Remove the pan from the heat.

2 Stir in the liqueur, if using, the sugar and vanilla extract. Serve warm.

BASIC RECIPES

Dark Chocolate Ganache

PREPARATION TIME: 5 minutes, plus cooling
COOKING TIME: 5 minutes

MAKES: 250ml/
9fl oz/1 cup

175g/6oz dark
   (bittersweet) chocolate,
   broken into pieces
25g/1oz/2 tbsp butter
125ml/4fl oz/½ cup
   double (heavy) cream

1 In a small saucepan, combine all of the ingredients over a low heat and stir until the chocolate and butter have melted. Remove the pan from the heat.

2 Pour into a heatproof bowl and leave to cool for around 20 minutes, or until the mixture begins to thicken. Use as a filling or topping in your chosen cake recipe, or serve warm as a sauce.

**BASIC
RECIPES**

Creamy Chocolate Frosting

PREPARATION TIME: 10 minutes

**MAKES: 250ml/
9fl oz/ 1 cup**

225g/8oz/1¾ cups
   icing (confectioners')
   sugar
3 tbsp unsweetened
   cocoa powder
25g/1oz/2 tbsp
   butter, melted
4–5 tbsp milk

1 Sift the icing sugar and cocoa into a bowl.

2 Stir in the melted butter and enough of the milk to make a creamy consistency.

3 Use immediately.

Shiny Chocolate Frosting

PREPARATION TIME: 15 minutes

MAKES: 250ml/ 9fl oz/ 1 cup

400g/14oz/3 cups
  icing (confectioners')
  sugar
2 tbsp unsweetened
  cocoa powder
15g/½oz/1 tbsp
  butter, softened

1 Place the icing sugar and cocoa in a bowl and make a small well in the middle. Place the butter in the well and pour over 2½ tbsp boiling water.

2 Stir until the butter has melted, then continue stirring until the frosting is of spreading consistency, adding about another 2½ tbsp boiling water as required.

3 Use immediately.

BASIC
RECIPES

Rich Chocolate Ice Cream

PREPARATION TIME: 20 minutes, plus chilling and churning
COOKING TIME: 10 minutes

MAKES: 1l/35fl oz/
4¼ cups

300ml/10½fl oz/
  1¼ cups milk
300ml/10½fl oz/
  1¼ cups double
  (heavy) cream
350g/12oz dark
  (bittersweet) or milk
  chocolate, broken
  into pieces
4 egg yolks
100g/3½oz/½ cup
  caster (granulated) sugar

1 In a small saucepan, heat the milk, cream and chocolate together over a low heat until the chocolate has just melted. Remove the pan from the heat and stir with a wooden spoon until smooth.

2 In a large, heatproof bowl, beat the egg yolks and sugar together using a hand whisk, then pour in the hot chocolate mixture, whisking constantly. Return the mixture to the saucepan and heat, stirring constantly with a wooden spoon, until the mixture just begins to thicken and lightly coats the back of the spoon. Do not allow the mixture to boil as it will curdle.

3 Remove from the heat, pour into a clean heatproof bowl and leave to cool completely. Refrigerate for 3 hours or overnight, then churn in an ice-cream machine according to the manufacturer's instructions.

AMERICAS

Chocolate Semifreddos

PREPARATION TIME: 30 minutes, plus freezing

SERVES: 8

3 egg yolks
1 egg
100g/3½oz/½ cup caster (granulated) sugar
2 tsp dark rum
225g/8oz dark (bittersweet) chocolate, melted and cooled slightly
250ml/9fl oz/1 cup double (heavy) cream, whipped to soft peaks
50g/1¾oz/½ cup finely chopped toasted hazelnuts
fresh fruit, to serve (optional)
2 tbsp melted chocolate, to serve (optional)
handful cocoa beans, to serve (optional)

1 Using an electric hand mixer, whisk together the egg yolks, egg, sugar and rum in a heatproof bowl over a pan of just simmering water. Whisk until thick and creamy.

2 Remove from the heat and fold in the melted chocolate, cream and toasted hazelnuts.

3 Spoon evenly into 8 x 100ml/3½fl oz/scant ½ cup silicone moulds (or one large mould lined with cling film/plastic wrap) and freeze for at least 4 hours before gently turning out.

4 Serve as desired. You can select your choice of fresh fruit or drizzle the plate with melted chocolate and serve with a few cocoa beans.

Mississippi Mud Cake

PREPARATION TIME: 35 minutes
COOKING TIME: 60–65 minutes

MAKES: 1 x 23cm/
9in cake

200g/7oz/¾ cup plus
  2 tbsp butter, chopped,
  plus extra for greasing
100g/3½oz dark
  (bittersweet) chocolate,
  broken into pieces
300g/10½oz/1½ cups
  caster (granulated) sugar
2 tbsp whisky
150g/5½oz/1 cup plus
  2 tbsp plain (all-purpose)
  flour
1 tbsp self-raising flour
2 tbsp unsweetened cocoa
  powder
2 eggs, lightly beaten

1 Preheat the oven to 170°C/325°F/gas 3. Grease a 23cm/9in spring-form cake pan with butter, and line the base with baking paper.

2 In a small saucepan, gently heat the butter, chocolate, sugar, whisky and 150ml/5fl oz/⅔ cup water together over a low heat until the chocolate has just melted. Pour into a heatproof bowl and stir with a wooden spoon until smooth, then set aside to cool for 10 minutes. In a separate bowl, mix the flours and cocoa together, then fold into the chocolate mixture with the eggs. Pour into the prepared pan.

3 Bake in the hot oven for 55–60 minutes, or until a skewer inserted into the middle of the cake comes out slightly moist. Remove from the oven and leave in the pan to cool for 15 minutes, then turn out on to a wire (cooling) rack to cool completely.

FOR THE CHOCOLATE FUDGE FROSTING

75g/2¾oz dark (bittersweet) chocolate, broken into pieces

75g/2¾oz/5 tbsp butter, chopped

250g/9oz/2 cups icing (confectioners') sugar

2 tbsp unsweetened cocoa powder

5 tbsp milk

1 tsp vanilla extract

4 To make the chocolate fudge frosting, in a small saucepan, heat the chocolate and butter over a low heat until just melted. In a medium-size bowl, mix the icing sugar and cocoa together, then pour the melted chocolate over. Add the milk and vanilla extract and stir to combine well.

5 Put the bowl containing the mixture into a larger bowl containing a little iced water and beat the mixture with a wooden spoon until it is thick enough to spread and hold its shape.

6 To ice the cake, use a palette knife to spread over the chocolate fudge frosting.

VARIATION
If you don't have an angel
cake pan, use a 20cm/8in
round pan, but make only half
of the recipe.

Chocolate Angel Food Cake

PREPARATION TIME: 15 minutes
COOKING TIME: 45–50 minutes

MAKES: 1 x 21 x
10cm/8¼ x 4in cake

6 eggs, separated
250ml/9fl oz/1 cup
   vegetable oil
150g/5½oz/1¼ cups
   drinking chocolate
280g/10oz/2¼ cups
   self-raising flour
400g/14oz/1½ cups
   plus 4 tbsp caster
   (granulated) sugar
icing (confectioners') sugar,
   sifted, for dusting

1 Preheat the oven to 150°C/300°F/gas 2.
Place an ungreased, loose-bottomed angel cake
pan on a baking tray.

2 Place the egg yolks, oil, drinking chocolate,
flour, caster sugar and 250ml/9fl oz/1 cup
water in a large bowl and mix on low speed with
an electric hand mixer until just combined. Then
beat at the highest setting for 10 minutes.

3 In a clean bowl, whisk the egg whites until stiff,
then fold gently into the chocolate mixture using
a metal spoon. Pour into the prepared pan.

4 Bake in the hot oven for 45–50 minutes, or
until the cake is firm. Remove from the oven and
turn the pan upside down on a wire (cooling)
rack, then leave in the pan to cool. When cold,
loosen the cake from the pan with a sharp knife,
turn out on to a plate and dust with icing sugar.

AMERICAS

Caribbean Chocolate Rum Cake

PREPARATION TIME: 30 minutes
COOKING TIME: 45–50 minutes

MAKES: 1 x 23cm/
9in cake

150g/5½oz/⅔ cup butter,
  softened, plus extra for
  greasing
250g/9oz/1¼ cups
  caster (granulated) sugar
6 medium eggs, lightly
  beaten
2 tbsp dark rum
225g/8oz dark
  (bittersweet) chocolate,
  melted and cooled
  slightly
225g/8oz/2 cups
  ground almonds
3 tbsp chopped candied
  stem ginger

1 Preheat the oven to 180°C/350°F/gas 4. Grease a 23cm/9in springform cake tin with butter and line the base with baking paper.

2 Cream the butter with the sugar using an electric hand mixer until light and fluffy. Add the lightly beaten eggs gradually, beating well between additions. Stir in the rum, cooled chocolate and the ground almonds. Fold in the chopped stem ginger, then pour into the prepared pan.

3 Bake in the hot oven for 40–45 minutes, or until the cake is firm and a skewer inserted into the middle of the cake comes out clean. Remove from the oven and leave the cake in the pan to cool for 10 minutes, then turn out on to a wire (cooling) rack to cool completely.

FOR THE CHOCOLATE RUM FROSTING

100g/3½oz dark (bittersweet) chocolate, broken into pieces

25g/1oz/2 tbsp butter, chopped

300g/10½oz/2⅓ cups icing (confectioners') sugar

100ml/3½fl oz/scant ½ cup double (heavy) cream

2 tbsp dark or light rum

1 tsp vanilla extract

4 While the cake is cooling, make the chocolate rum frosting. In a small saucepan, combine the chocolate and butter together over a low heat and stir until smooth.

5 Place the icing sugar in a large, heatproof bowl and, using a wooden spoon, mix in the chocolate mixture, cream, rum and vanilla extract. Whisk until thick using an electric hand mixer.

6 When the cake is cold, ice the cake with the chocolate rum frosting.

Chocolate Fudge Cake

PREPARATION TIME: 15 minutes
COOKING TIME: 25–30 minutes

MAKES: 1 x 23cm/
9in cake

75g/2¾oz/5 tbsp butter,
  melted, plus extra for
  greasing
200g/7oz/1 cup soft
  brown sugar
2 eggs, lightly beaten
1 tsp vanilla extract
140g/5oz/1¼ cups self-
  raising flour
2 tbsp unsweetened cocoa
  powder
1 recipe quantity Creamy
  Chocolate Frosting
  (see page 28)

1 Preheat the oven to 180°C/350°F/gas 4.
Grease a 23cm/9in spring-form cake pan with
butter and line the base with baking paper.

2 In a large bowl, beat the butter and sugar
together using an electric hand mixer, then beat in
the eggs and vanilla extract until well combined.

3 In another bowl, combine the flour and cocoa,
then add to the sugar mixture with 125ml/4fl oz/
½ cup hot water, stirring with a wooden spoon until
everything is moist. Pour into the prepared pan.

4 Bake in the hot oven for 25–30 minutes, or until
a skewer inserted into the middle of the cake comes
out clean. Remove from the oven and leave the
cake in the pan to cool for 10 minutes, then turn out
on to a wire (cooling) rack to cool completely.

5 To frost the cake, use a palette knife to spread
over the creamy chocolate frosting.

Chocolate Banana Bread

PREPARATION TIME: 15 minutes
COOKING TIME: 50–55 minutes

MAKES: 1 x 24 x
12cm/9½ x 4½in loaf

125g/4½oz/½ cup
butter, softened, plus
extra for greasing and
to serve
125g/4½oz/⅔ cup soft
brown sugar
2 eggs, lightly beaten
150g/5½oz dark
(bittersweet) chocolate,
melted and left to cool
3 ripe bananas, peeled
and mashed, plus 1 small
banana, peeled and cut
in ½ legnthways
1 tsp vanilla extract
200g/7oz/1½ cups
self-raising flour

1 Preheat the oven to 180°C/350°F/gas 4.
Grease a 24 x 12cm/9½ x 4½in loaf pan with
butter, and line the base with baking paper.

2 In a large bowl, beat the butter and sugar
together until light and fluffy using an electric
hand mixer. Add the eggs, beating well, then stir
in the melted chocolate, bananas, vanilla extract
and flour until just combined using a wooden
spoon. Spoon into the prepared pan. Place the
two banana halves on top of the cake batter,
pressing lightly so that they adhere to the cake.

3 Bake in the hot oven for 50–55 minutes, or
until a skewer inserted into the middle of the cake
comes out with just a few crumbs clinging to it.
Remove from the oven and leave the cake in the
pan to cool for 10 minutes, then turn out on to
a wire (cooling) rack to cool completely. Serve
in slices with butter for spreading.

AMERICAS

Sopapillas (Mexican Donuts)

PREPARATION TIME: 20 minutes, plus resting
COOKING TIME: 20 minutes

MEXICO

MAKES: 16 sopapillas

250g/9oz/2 cups plain
(all-purpose) flour, plus
extra for dusting
1 tsp baking powder
¼ tsp salt
25g/1oz/2 tbsp butter,
chilled and cut into small
pieces
vegetable oil, for frying
30g/1oz/¼ cup caster
sugar, sifted
2 tsp ground cinnamon
1 recipe quantity Rich
Chocolate Sauce (see
page 25), to serve

1 Sift the flour and baking powder into a bowl with the salt. Add the butter and rub into the flour until the mixture resembles fine breadcrumbs.

2 Mix in 500ml/17fl oz/2 cups of hot water gradually using a flat knife until a soft dough forms. Place the dough on a lightly floured surface and knead for 2–3 minutes until smooth. Wrap in cling film (plastic wrap) and leave to rest for 30 minutes.

3 Roll out the dough and cut into 16 pieces (can be triangles or rectangles). Heat the oil in a pan to 180°C/350°F. Gently place each dough shape into the pan. (You may need to cook them in batches.) They will puff up quickly – cook until light brown (around 2 minutes), then turn over and cook for a further 2 minutes. Remove from the oil and drain, then cool.

4 Mix the caster sugar and cinnamon and dust the cooled sopapillas. Serve with chocolate sauce.

Chocolate Fudge Brownies

PREPARATION TIME: 20 minutes
COOKING TIME: 20–25 minutes

MAKES: 12 brownies

200g/7oz/¾ cup plus
  2 tbsp butter, chopped,
  plus extra for greasing
200g/7oz dark
  (bittersweet) chocolate,
  broken into pieces
250g/9oz/1¼ cups
  caster (granulated) sugar
3 eggs, lightly beaten
1 tsp vanilla extract
125g/4½oz/1 cup plain
  (all-purpose) flour
pinch salt

1 Preheat the oven to 180°C/350°F/gas 4. Grease a shallow 23cm/9in square cake pan with butter and line the base with baking paper, leaving some hanging over the edges to make removing the brownies easier.

2 In a medium-size saucepan, melt the butter and chocolate over a low heat until the chocolate has just melted, stirring constantly with a wooden spoon, then remove the pan from the heat. Add the sugar and mix well, then leave to cool to room temperature. In a large bowl, gradually mix the eggs into the chocolate mixture with the vanilla extract, then fold in the flour and salt using a metal spoon. Pour the mixture into the prepared pan.

3 Bake in the hot oven for 15–20 minutes, or until the brownie is firm around the edges and still slightly soft in the middle. Remove from the oven and leave in the pan to cool completely, then cut into 12 squares.

Dark & White Chocolate Brownies

PREPARATION TIME: 20 minutes
COOKING TIME: 20–25 minutes

MAKES: 12 brownies

175g/6oz/¾ cup butter, chopped, plus extra for greasing
2 tbsp unsweetened cocoa powder
300g/10½oz/1½ cups caster (granulated) sugar
2 eggs, lightly beaten
1 tsp vanilla extract
150g/5½oz/1 cup plus 2 tbsp plain (all-purpose) flour
60g/2¼oz white chocolate chips
60g/2¼oz dark (bittersweet) chocolate chips
60g/2¼oz/⅔ cup walnuts, roughly chopped

1 Preheat the oven to 180°C/350°F/gas 4. Grease a shallow 23cm/9in square cake pan with butter and line the base with baking paper, leaving some hanging over the edges to make removing the brownies easier.

2 In a large saucepan, heat the butter with the cocoa and sugar over a low heat until just melted, then remove from the heat and set aside to cool. When cool, add all the remaining ingredients and stir with a wooden spoon until just combined. Pour into the prepared pan.

3 Bake in the hot oven for 15–20 minutes, or until the brownie is firm around the edges and still slightly soft in the middle. Remove from the oven and leave in the pan to cool completely, then cut into 12 squares.

Rocky Road Brownies

PREPARATION TIME: 20 minutes, plus setting
COOKING TIME: 20–25 minutes

MAKES: 12 brownies

175g/6oz/¾ cup butter,
   chopped, plus extra for
   greasing
2 tbsp unsweetened cocoa
   powder
250g/9oz/1¼ cups caster
   (granulated) sugar
2 eggs, lightly beaten
1 tsp vanilla extract
150g/5½oz/1 cup plus
   2 tbsp plain (all-purpose)
   flour
100g/3½oz dark
   (bittersweet) or milk
   chocolate chips
200g/7oz white and pink
   marshmallows, chopped
1 recipe quantity Shiny
   Chocolate Frosting
   (see page 29)

1 Preheat the oven to 180°C/350°F/gas 4. Grease a shallow 23cm/9in square cake pan with butter and line with baking paper.

2 In a saucepan, heat the butter with the cocoa and sugar over a low heat until melted. Remove from the heat and set aside to cool. When cool, add the eggs, vanilla extract, flour and chocolate chips and stir with a wooden spoon until just combined. Pour the mixture into the prepared pan.

3 Bake in the hot oven for 15–20 minutes, or until the edges of the brownie are firm and the middle is still moist. Remove from the oven and leave the brownie in the pan to cool completely.

4 In a bowl, stir the marshmallows into the shiny chocolate frosting until they are well coated, then spread the mixture evenly over the top of the brownie. Leave the frosting to set for 30 minutes, then cut the brownie into 12 squares.

Chocolate Brownie Cookies

PREPARATION TIME: 20 minutes
COOKING TIME: 11–13 minutes

MAKES: 12 cookies

25g/1oz/2 tbsp butter,
  chopped, plus extra for
  greasing
175g/6oz dark
  (bittersweet) chocolate,
  broken into pieces
1 egg, lightly beaten
100g/3½oz/½ cup
  caster (granulated) sugar
1 tsp vanilla extract
40g/1½oz/⅓ cup
  self-raising flour
60g/2¼oz/⅔ cup
  pecan nuts, toasted
  and chopped
85g/3oz/½ cup milk
  chocolate chips
small handful of sea salt,
  to garnish

1 Preheat the oven to 180°C/350°F/gas 4. Grease 2 large baking trays with butter.

2 In a small saucepan, melt the butter and chocolate together over a low heat, stirring with a wooden spoon until smooth. Remove the pan from the heat and set aside to cool. In a large bowl, beat the egg and sugar together until thick and creamy, using an electric hand mixer. Stir in the melted chocolate mixture, vanilla extract, flour and nuts using a wooden spoon. Finally mix in the chocolate chips. Place tablespoonfuls of the mixture on the prepared baking trays, leaving approximately 10cm/4in between them to allow for spreading.

3 Bake in the hot oven for 6–8 minutes, or until the cookies are puffed and cracked, but still moist. Remove the cookies from the oven and transfer them to a wire (cooling) rack to cool completely. Garnish each cookie with a pinch of sea salt.

AMERICAS

Chocolate & Peanut Butter Cookies

PREPARATION TIME: 20 minutes, plus chilling
COOKING TIME: 10–12 minutes

MAKES: 18 cookies

125g/4½oz/½ cup butter,
  softened, plus extra for
  greasing
125g/4½oz/½ cup plus
  2 tbsp caster (granulated)
  sugar
125g/4½oz/½ cup
  crunchy peanut butter
2 tbsp golden (light corn)
  syrup
1 tbsp milk
175g/6oz/1¼ cups plain
  (all-purpose) flour
2 tbsp unsweetened cocoa
  powder
½ tsp bicarbonate of soda
  (baking soda)

1 In a large bowl, beat together the butter and sugar until light and creamy using an electric hand mixer. Mix in all the remaining ingredients with a wooden spoon into a well blended dough. Shape the dough into a log measuring approximately 30 x 4cm/12 x 1½in and wrap in cling film (plastic wrap). Refrigerate for 1 hour until firm but not solid.

2 Preheat the oven to 180°C/350°F/gas 4. Grease 2 large baking trays with butter.

3 Cut the dough into 18 slices, each about 5mm/¼in thick, and place the slices on the prepared trays, leaving approximately 5cm/2in of space between them to allow for spreading.

4 Bake in the hot oven for 10–12 minutes, or until the cookies are firm. Remove the cookies from the oven and leave to cool on the trays for 10 minutes, then transfer to a wire (cooling) rack to cool completely.

Chocolate Alfajores

PREPARATION TIME: 30 minutes, plus chilling
COOKING TIME: 7–8 minutes

ARGENTINA

MAKES: 16 biscuits

90g/3¼oz/¾ cup plain (all-purpose) flour, plus extra for dusting
100g/3½oz/1 cup cornflour (cornstarch)
20g/¾oz/2 tbsp unsweetened cocoa powder
½ tsp baking powder
125g/4½oz/½ cup butter, softened
75g/2¾oz/⅓ cup caster (granulated) sugar
3 egg yolks
200g/7oz dulche de leche
½ recipe quantity Shiny Chocolate Frosting (see page 29)

1 Sift together the flour, cornflour, cocoa powder and baking powder in a bowl.

2 In a separate large bowl, beat together the butter and sugar until light and fluffy using an electric hand mixer, then beat in the egg yolks. Add the sifted flour mixture approximately one-third at a time and mix well to form a dough. Wrap in cling film (plastic wrap) and refrigerate for 30 minutes.

3 Preheat the oven to 180°C/350°F/gas 4. Line a large baking tray with baking paper.

4 Roll out the dough on a lightly floured surface to approximately 5mm/¼in thick. Cut the dough into 32 biscuits using a 5cm/2in pastry cutter and place on the prepared baking trays. Bake for 7–8 minutes, or until just set. Leave to cool completely on a wire (cooling) rack.

100g/3½oz/1 cup desiccated (dried shredded) coconut, toasted

5 Spread the frosting over the top of half of the biscuits and let the icing set. Sandwich 1 heaped tsp of the dulce de leche between two biscuits (one with icing and one without) and squeeze gently. Smooth the sides with a knife and roll in the toasted coconut. Repeat for all the biscuits. Refrigerate for 10 minutes to set the caramel.

Chocolate Chip Pecan Cookies

PREPARATION TIME: 20 minutes
COOKING TIME: 10–12 minutes

MAKES: 30 cookies

140g/5oz/½ cup plus 2
tbsp butter, softened, plus
extra for greasing
40g/1½oz/3 tbsp caster
(granulated) sugar
60g/2¼oz/⅓ cup soft
brown sugar
1 egg, lightly beaten
125g/4½oz/1 cup plain
(all-purpose) flour
½ tsp bicarbonate of soda
(baking soda)
150g/5½oz/scant 1 cup
dark (bittersweet) or milk
chocolate chips
100g/3½oz/1 cup pecan
nuts, finely chopped

1 Preheat the oven to 180°C/350°F/gas 4.
Grease 2 large baking trays with butter.

2 In a large bowl, beat the butter and both sugars
together until light and creamy using an electric
hand mixer, then beat in the egg. In a separate
bowl, mix all the remaining ingredients together
using a wooden spoon, then stir into the butter
mixture until well combined.

3 Form the mixture into roughly 30 balls the size
of teaspoons. Place on the prepared trays, leaving
around 5cm/2in of space between them. Press
down lightly to flatten the balls into rounds.

4 Bake in the hot oven for 10–12 minutes until the
cookies are lightly browned. (You may need to
cook them in batches.) Remove the cookies from
the oven and leave on the baking trays to cool
for 10 minutes, then transfer the cookies to wire
(cooling) racks to cool completely.

Double Chocolate Muffins

PREPARATION TIME: 15 minutes
COOKING TIME: 20–25 minutes

MAKES: 12 muffins

125g/4½oz/½ cup
  butter, melted, plus extra
  for greasing
375g/13oz/3 cups self-
  raising flour
3 tbsp unsweetened cocoa
  powder
175g/6oz/¾ cup plus
  2 tbsp caster (granulated)
  sugar
2 eggs, lightly beaten
125g/4½oz dark
  (bittersweet) or milk
  chocolate chips
250ml/9fl oz/1 cup milk

1 Preheat the oven to 190°C/375°F/gas 5. Grease a 12-hole muffin pan with butter.

2 In a large bowl, mix together all the ingredients until just combined using a wooden spoon. Don't overmix! Divide the mixture evenly between the prepared pan holes.

3 Bake in the hot oven for 20–25 minutes until the muffins have risen and a toothpick inserted in the centre comes out clean. Remove from the oven and leave in the pan to cool for 5–10 minutes, then remove from the pan and transfer to a wire (cooling) rack to cool completely.

White Chocolate & Blueberry Muffins

PREPARATION TIME: 15 minutes
COOKING TIME: 15–20 minutes

MAKES: 12 muffins

125g/4½oz/½ cup butter,
  melted, plus extra for
  greasing
250g/9oz/2 cups self-
  raising flour
100g/3½oz/½ cup caster
  (granulated) sugar
125g/4½oz white
  chocolate, broken into
  pieces
1 egg, lightly beaten
125ml/4fl oz/½ cup milk
1 tsp vanilla extract
150g/5½oz/heaped
  1 cup blueberries

1 Preheat the oven to 190°C/375°F/gas 5.
Grease a 12-hole muffin pan with butter.

2 In a large bowl, mix all the ingredients together
until just combined using a wooden spoon. Don't
overmix! Divide the mixture evenly between the
prepared pan holes.

3 Bake in the hot oven for 15–20 minutes until the
muffins have risen and are golden brown. Remove
from the oven and leave the muffins in the pan
to cool for 5–10 minutes, then remove from
the pan and transfer to a wire (cooling) rack
to cool completely.

Chocolate Baked Alaska

PREPARATION TIME: 15 minutes
COOKING TIME: 4–5 minutes

SERVES 6

1 recipe quantity
  Chocolate Fudge
  Brownies, baked in a
  20cm/8in round cake
  pan (see page 48)
3 egg whites
125g/4½oz/½ cup
  plus 2 tbsp caster
  (superfine) sugar
pinch cream of tartar
1l/34fl oz/4 cups Rich
  Chocolate Ice Cream
  (see page 30), slightly
  softened

1 Preheat the oven to 230°C/450°F/gas 8. Place the brownie (uncut) on a kitchen foil-lined baking tray.

2 In a large bowl, whisk the egg whites to stiff peaks using an electric hand mixer, then whisk in the sugar and cream of tartar until the meringue is thick and shiny.

3 Scoop the chocolate ice cream on to the top of the baked brownie, smoothing down in a rounded curve. Spread the meringue over the sides and top of the ice-cream cake, so that the ice cream is completely covered. Bake in the very hot oven for 4–5 minutes until the meringue is lightly browned.

4 Remove the baked Alaska from the oven and serve immediately.

Raspberry Ripple White Chocolate Cheesecake

PREPARATION TIME: 25 minutes, plus chilling
COOKING TIME: 45–50 minutes

MAKES: 1 x 23cm/
9in cheesecake

butter, for greasing
1 recipe quantity Chocolate
   Crumb Crust (see page 18)
500g/1lb 2oz/2¼ cups
   cream cheese, softened
200g/7oz/1 cup caster
   (granulated) sugar
2 tbsp plain (all-purpose)
   flour
4 eggs, lightly beaten
250g/9oz white chocolate,
   melted and left to cool
2 tsp vanilla extract
125ml/4fl oz/½ cup
   double (heavy) cream
125g/4½oz/1 cup
   raspberries, puréed

1 Preheat the oven to 180°C/350°F/gas 4. Grease a 23cm/9in spring-form cake pan with butter and press in the chocolate crumb crust.

2 In a large bowl, beat the cream cheese and sugar together until light and creamy using an electric hand mixer. Add the flour, eggs, melted chocolate and vanilla extract and beat until just combined. Stir in the cream. Gently swirl through the raspberry purée using a wooden spoon. Pour the filling mixture over the crumb crust base.

3 Bake in the hot oven for 45–50 minutes, or until the cheesecake is firm around the edges but still slightly wobbly in the middle. Remove from the oven and leave in the pan to cool completely.

4 Refrigerate the cheesecake for 2 hours or overnight, then remove from the pan to serve.

Baked Bananas with Chocolate Rum Sauce

PREPARATION TIME: 10 minutes
COOKING TIME: 17–20 minutes

CARIBBEAN

SERVES 4

butter, for greasing
4 ripe bananas, peeled and
  halved lengthways
200ml/7fl oz/scant 1 cup
  double (heavy) cream
50g/1¾oz/¼ cup soft
  brown sugar
2 tbsp unsweetened cocoa
  powder

**FOR THE CHOCOLATE
RUM SAUCE**
250ml/9fl oz/1 cup
  double (heavy) cream
2 tsp granulated sugar
100g/3½oz dark
  (bittersweet) chocolate
2 tbsp dark rum

1 Preheat the oven to 180°C/350°F/gas 4. Grease an ovenproof ceramic dish with butter. Arrange the bananas in the prepared dish.

2 In a small saucepan, whisk the cream, sugar and cocoa together over a low heat until hot, then pour over the bananas.

3 Bake in the hot oven for 12–15 minutes, or until the bananas are soft.

4 Meanwhile, make the chocolate rum sauce. In a small saucepan, heat the cream, sugar and chocolate (broken into pieces) together over a low heat until the chocolate has melted, stirring with a wooden spoon until smooth. Remove the pan from the heat and stir in the rum.

5 Once baked, remove the bananas from the oven and serve warm with the chocolate rum sauce.

Grasshopper Pie

PREPARATION TIME: 20 minutes, plus chilling
COOKING TIME: 5 minutes

MAKES: 1 x 23cm/
9in pie

4 sheets leaf gelatine
2 tbsp crème de menthe
   liqueur
100g/3½oz dark
   (bittersweet) chocolate,
   chopped, plus 3 tbsp
   grated to garnish
2 egg whites
45g/1½oz/scant ¼ cup
   caster (superfine) sugar
250ml/9fl oz/1 cup
   double (heavy) cream,
   whipped to soft peaks
3 tbsp finely chopped mint
   leaves
1 Chocolate Crumb Crust,
   baked (see page 18)

1 Soak the gelatine sheets in cold water for 5–10 minutes until soft, then wring out any excess water.

2 In a small saucepan, heat the crème de menthe over a low heat, then add the soaked gelatine. Remove from the heat and stir with a metal spoon until the gelatine is dissolved. Set aside to cool.

3 Melt the chopped dark chocolate, then set aside to cool but not set.

4 In a large bowl, whisk the egg whites to soft peaks using an electric hand mixer, then add the sugar gradually, whisking until stiff. Using a metal spoon, fold the whipped cream into the egg whites with the gelatine, melted chocolate and mint.

5 Pour the mixture into the chocolate crumb crust and smooth the top. Sprinkle over the grated chocolate. Refrigerate for 2 hours, or until set.

Chocolate Pear Upside-down Cake

PREPARATION TIME: 20 minutes
COOKING TIME: 30–35 minutes

MAKES: 1 x 23cm/
9in cake

200g/7oz/¾ cup plus
   2 tbsp butter, softened,
   plus extra for greasing
200g/7oz dark
   (bittersweet) chocolate,
   broken into pieces
150g/5½oz/¾ cup caster
   (granulated) sugar
3 eggs, lightly beaten
1 tsp vanilla extract
100g/3½oz/¾ cup
   self-raising flour
40g/1½oz/3 tbsp soft
   brown sugar
3 pears, ripe but firm,
   peeled, cored and sliced
   into quarters

1 Preheat the oven to 180°C/350°F/gas 4. Grease a 23cm/9in spring-form cake pan with butter and line the base with baking paper.

2 In a small saucepan, combine the butter, chocolate and caster sugar over a low heat until just melted, stirring with a wooden spoon. Remove from the heat and set aside to cool completely. Once cool, stir in the eggs, vanilla extract and flour until just combined.

3 Sprinkle the brown sugar over the base of the prepared pan, arrange the pear quarters over the top, then pour over the chocolate batter.

4 Bake in the hot oven for 25–30 minutes, or until a skewer inserted into the middle of the cake comes out with just a few moist crumbs on it. Remove from the oven and leave the cake in the pan to cool for 15 minutes, then turn out on to a wire (cooling) rack to cool completely, pear-side up.

Chocolate Raisin & Rum Ice Cream

PREPARATION TIME: 15 minutes, plus chilling and churning
COOKING TIME: 5 minutes

MAKES: 1l/35fl oz/
4¼ cups

60g/2¼oz/½ cup raisins
1½ tbsp dark rum
100g/3½oz/½ cup caster
  (granulated) sugar
250ml/9fl oz/1 cup milk
400ml/14fl oz/1⅔ cups
  double (heavy) cream
2 tsp vanilla extract
100g/3½oz dark
  (bittersweet) chocolate,
  grated

1 Place the raisins and rum in a small bowl and microwave on high for 30 seconds. Set aside to cool completely.

2 In a medium-size saucepan, heat the sugar and milk together over a low heat until the sugar has dissolved. Remove from the heat and stir in the cream. Pour into a bowl and leave to cool completely. Refrigerate for 3 hours or overnight.

3 When cold, stir in the rum-soaked raisins, vanilla extract and grated chocolate, then churn in an ice-cream machine according to the manufacturer's instructions.

Chocolate Pear Sundaes with Roasted Almonds

PREPARATION TIME: 20 minutes
COOKING TIME: 5 minutes

SERVES 4

100g/3½oz/½ cup caster
  (granulated) sugar
4 ripe pears
8 scoops Rich Chocolate
  Ice Cream (see page 30),
  slightly softened
1 recipe quantity Double
  Chocolate Sauce
  (see page 24)
20g/¾oz flaked (sliced)
  almonds, roasted, to serve

1 In a small saucepan, heat the sugar and 100ml/3½fl oz/scant ½ cup water together over a medium heat until the sugar has dissolved, stirring frequently with a metal spoon.

2 Peel the pears and cut in half vertically, keeping the stalks intact if possible. Remove the seeds and core using a melon baller to create a neat shape. Toss the halved pears in the warm sugar syrup until lightly coated.

3 Divide the pears and syrup between 4 serving dishes. Place 2 scoops of ice cream on each dish and spoon over the double chocolate sauce. Sprinkle with the flaked almonds and serve.

Chocolate Milkshakes

PREPARATION TIME: 5 minutes

SERVES 4

500ml/17fl oz/2 cups
  cold milk
1 tsp vanilla extract
4 tbsp Double Chocolate
  Sauce, plus extra for
  serving (see page 24)
8 tbsp Rich Chocolate Ice
  Cream (see page 30)
4 tablespoons whipped
  cream, to serve

1 Add all of the ingredients to a blender and blend together until well combined.

2 Divide the milkshake mixture equally between 4 glasses.

3 Add whipped cream and an extra drizzle of chocolate sauce before serving.

ASIA PACIFIC

Chocolate Butterfly Cakes

PREPARATION TIME: 20 minutes
COOKING TIME: 15–20 minutes

MAKES: 12 cakes

125g/4½oz/½ cup
  butter, softened
125g/4½oz/½ cup plus
  2 tbsp caster (granulated)
  sugar
2 eggs, lightly beaten
1 tsp vanilla extract
200g/7oz/1½ cups
  self-raising flour
2 tbsp unsweetened cocoa
  powder
3 tbsp milk
1 recipe quantity
  Chocolate Chantilly
  Cream (see page 19)
icing (confectioners') sugar,
  sifted, for dusting

1 Preheat the oven to 180°C/350°F/gas 4.
Place 12 cupcake cases into a 12-hole muffin pan.

2 In a large bowl, beat the butter and sugar
together until light and fluffy using an electric
hand mixer, then gradually beat in the eggs and
vanilla extract until combined. In a clean bowl,
sift the flour and cocoa together, then fold into the
mixture with the milk using a metal spoon. Divide
the batter evenly between the cupcake cases.

3 Bake in the hot oven for 15–20 minutes, or until
the cakes are firm to the touch. Remove from the
oven and tranfer to a wire (cooling) rack to cool.

4 Cut off a small circle at the top of each cake. Cut
the circle in half to form two semi-circular pieces.
Place a spoonful of the chocolate cream in the
middle of each cake, then add the two semicircles
on top to form "wings" and dust with icing sugar.

ASIA
PACIFIC

White Chocolate, Lime & Coconut Cupcakes

PREPARATION TIME: 20 minutes, plus chilling
COOKING TIME: 18–20 minutes

MAKES: 12 cupcakes

150g/5½oz/1 cup plus
   2 tbsp self-raising flour
45g/1½oz/scant ¼ cup
   caster (granulated) sugar
50g/1¾oz/3½ tbsp
   butter, melted
1 egg, lightly beaten
100ml/3½fl oz/scant
   ½ cup milk
1 tsp vanilla extract
finely grated zest and
   juice of 1 lime
100g/3½oz white
   chocolate, broken into
   pieces
45g/1½oz/½ cup
   desiccated (dried
   shredded) coconut

1 Preheat the oven to 180°C/350°F/gas 4. Place 12 paper cake cases into the holes of a 12-hole muffin pan.

2 In a large bowl, combine the flour and sugar, and make a well in the middle. Mix together the melted butter, egg, milk, vanilla extract and lime zest and juice using a wooden spoon, then stir into the flour mixture until just combined. Stir in the white chocolate and coconut, then use a dessertspoon to divide the mixture evenly between the cake cases.

3 Bake in the hot oven for 18–20 minutes, or until the cakes are firm to the touch. Remove from the oven and transfer them to a wire (cooling) rack to cool completely.

FOR THE WHITE CHOCOLATE FROSTING

100g/3½oz white chocolate, broken into pieces
250ml/9fl oz/1 cup double (heavy) cream
250g/9oz/1 cup mascarpone cheese

4 Meanwhile, to make the white chocolate frosting, in a small saucepan, combine the chocolate and 150ml/5fl oz/⅔ cup of the cream over a low heat until the chocolate has just melted. Remove the pan from the heat and stir until smooth. Pour the mixture into a heatproof bowl and leave to cool for 30 minutes, stirring occasionally, then refrigerate for approximately 1 hour until cold.

5 In a separate large bowl, stir the mascarpone until smooth using a wooden spoon. Stir in the chocolate mixture and as much of the remaining cream as required to make a smooth spreading consistency.

6 To frost the cakes, use a palette knife to spread over the white chocolate frosting.

ASIA PACIFIC

Matcha & White Chocolate Blondies

PREPARATION TIME: 20 minutes
COOKING TIME: 22–25 minutes

MAKES: 16 blondies

100g/3½oz/7 tbsp
butter, chopped, plus
extra for greasing
125g/4½oz white
chocolate, in pieces
200g/7oz/1 cup caster
(granulated) sugar
3 eggs, lightly beaten
50g/1¾oz/½ cup
hazelnuts, skinned and
chopped
100g/3½oz white
chocolate chips
175g/6oz/1⅓ cups plain
(all-purpose) flour
1 tbsp matcha powder
80g icing (confectioners')
sugar, sifted

1 Preheat the oven to 180°C/350°F/gas 4. Grease a shallow 20cm/8in square cake pan with butter and line the base with baking paper.

2 In a saucepan, heat the butter and chocolate together over a low heat until the chocolate melts. Remove from the heat and stir gently until smooth.

3 In a large bowl, combine the sugar and eggs, then stir in the chocolate mixture, hazelnuts, chocolate chips, flour and matcha powder using a wooden spoon. Pour into the prepared pan.

4 Bake in the hot oven for 18–20 minutes, or until the cake is firm around the edges but still moist in the middle. Remove from the oven and leave the cake in the pan to cool completely. Remove the cake from the pan and cut into 16 squares. Mix together the icing sugar with 10ml warm water and drizzle over the brownies before serving.

Chocolate Macadamia Nut Tart

PREPARATION TIME: 40 minutes
COOKING TIME: 1 hour

AUSTRALIA

MAKES: 1 x 23cm/
9in tart

1 recipe quantity
  Chocolate Shortcrust
  Pastry (see pages 22–3)
plain (all-purpose) flour,
  for dusting
25g/1oz/2 tbsp butter,
  chopped
25g/1oz dark
  (bittersweet) chocolate,
  broken into pieces
2 eggs
65g/2¼oz/5 tbsp caster
  (granulated) sugar
200ml/7fl oz/scant
  1 cup clear honey
1 tsp vanilla extract

1 Preheat the oven to 180°C/350°F/gas 4.

2 Roll the pastry out on a lightly floured surface to around 5mm/¼in thick, and ease it into a 23cm/9in fluted, loose-bottomed flan pan, 3–4cm/1¼–1½in deep. Line the pastry case with baking paper and fill with baking beans (pie weights). Bake in the hot oven for 20 minutes.

3 Remove the paper and beans from the pastry case, then bake in the hot oven for a further 5–10 minutes, or until the pastry is dark brown.

4 For the filling, in a small saucepan, heat the butter and chocolate together over a low heat until just melted. Remove from the heat and set aside to cool.

EVERYBODY LOVES CHOCOLATE

200g/7oz/1¼ cups
  macadamia nuts, roughly
  chopped
icing (confectioners')
  sugar, sifted, for dusting
  (optional)

5 In a large bowl, beat the eggs and sugar together until light and creamy using an electric hand mixer, then beat in the honey, chocolate mixture and the vanilla extract. Stir in the nuts, then pour the filling into the prepared pastry case, being careful not to overfill.

6 Bake in the hot oven for 30–35 minutes, or until the filling is just firm. Remove from the oven and leave the tart in the pan to cool completely, then dust with icing sugar, if desired.

ASIA
PACIFIC

Chocolate Tart with Cardamom

PREPARATION TIME: 20 minutes
COOKING TIME: 25–30 minutes

MAKES: 1 x 23cm/ 9in tart

1 x 23cm/9in Sweet
  Shortcrust Pastry case,
  baked (see page 22)
50g/1¾oz/3½ tbsp
  butter
250g/9oz dark
  (bittersweet) chocolate,
  broken into pieces
3 eggs, separated
65g/2¼oz/5 tbsp caster
  (granulated) sugar
125ml/4fl oz/½ cup
  double (heavy) cream
1 tsp ground cardamom

1 Preheat the oven to 200°C/400°F/gas 6. Place the baked pastry case on a baking tray.

2 In a small saucepan, melt the butter and chocolate together over a low heat, then remove the pan from the heat and set aside to cool.

3 In a bowl, whisk the egg whites to soft peaks using an electric hand mixer, then gradually add the sugar, whisking until stiff. Beat the yolks into the chocolate mixture, then fold in the cream, cardamom and whisked egg whites, using a metal spoon until just combined. Pour the mixture into the baked pastry case, taking care not to overfill.

4 Bake in the hot oven for 20–25 minutes, or until the tart is just firm around the edges but the middle is still soft. Remove the tart from the oven and serve warm.

Chocolate Coconut Drops

PREPARATION TIME: 15 minutes
COOKING TIME: 10–12 minutes

MAKES: 20 biscuits

butter, for greasing
75g/2¾oz dark
  (bittersweet) chocolate,
  melted and left to cool
90g/3¼oz/1 cup
  desiccated (dried
  shredded) coconut
125g/4½oz/½ cup plus
  2 tbsp caster (granulated)
  sugar
1 tbsp unsweetened cocoa
  powder
1 egg white
1 tbsp icing (confectioners')
  sugar, sifted

1 Preheat the oven to 180°C/350°F/gas 4. Grease 2 baking trays with butter.

2 In a large bowl, mix together the melted chocolate, coconut, caster sugar, cocoa and egg white until well combined using a wooden spoon. Shape large teaspoonfuls of the mixture into balls and place them on the prepared baking trays, leaving approximately 5cm/2in of space between them to allow for spreading. Flatten each ball slightly, then sprinkle over the icing sugar.

3 Bake in the hot oven for 10–12 minutes, or until the biscuits are just firm. Remove from the oven and leave the biscuits to cool on the baking trays for 10 minutes, then transfer them to a wire (cooling) rack to cool completely.

ASIA PACIFIC

White Chocolate, Citrus & Coconut Truffles

PREPARATION TIME: 20 minutes, plus chilling
COOKING TIME: 5 minutes

MAKES: 30 truffles

100ml/3½fl oz/scant
  ½ cup coconut cream
350g/12oz white
  chocolate, broken into
  pieces
2 tsp finely grated
  lemon zest
2 tsp finely grated
  lime zest
2 tbsp coconut rum liqueur
90g/3¼oz/1 cup
  desiccated (dried
  shredded) coconut

1 In a small saucepan, combine the coconut cream and chocolate together over a low heat until just melted, stirring frequently with a wooden spoon. Remove from the heat and stir until smooth. Pour into a bowl and leave to cool, then stir in the lemon and lime zests and liqueur. Refrigerate for approximately 30 minutes until firm.

2 Roll teaspoonfuls of the mixture into balls and toss in the desiccated coconut to coat. Place on a baking tray lined with baking paper and refrigerate for 1 hour, or until firm.

Chocolate & Coconut Rough Slices

PREPARATION TIME: 20 minutes, plus chilling
COOKING TIME: 12–15 minutes

MAKES: 12 squares

125g/4½oz/½ cup
  butter, melted, plus extra
  for greasing
75g/2¾oz/½ cup plus
  1 tbsp self-raising flour
75g/2¾oz/½ cup plus
  1 tbsp plain (all-purpose)
  flour
2 tbsp unsweetened cocoa
  powder
65g/2¼oz/5 tbsp caster
  (granulated) sugar
45g/1½oz/½ cup
  desiccated (dried
  shredded) coconut

1 Preheat the oven to 180°C/350°F/gas 4.
Grease a shallow 23cm/9in square cake pan
with butter and line with baking paper.

2 In a large bowl, sift both flours and the cocoa
together, then add the sugar and coconut. Add
the melted butter and stir with a wooden spoon
until well combined. Press the mixture into the
prepared pan.

3 Bake in the hot oven for 12–15 minutes, or until
the cake is just firm. Remove from the oven and
leave in the pan to cool completely.

92   **EVERYBODY LOVES CHOCOLATE**

FOR THE TOPPING

100g/3½oz/¾ cup icing (confectioners') sugar

2 tbsp unsweetened cocoa powder

45g/1½oz/½ cup desiccated (dried shredded) coconut

125ml/4fl oz/½ cup condensed milk

4 For the topping, sift the icing sugar and cocoa together into a bowl, add the remaining ingredients and stir to combine. Spread the topping evenly over the baked cake slice using a palette knife. Refrigerate the iced cake for 30 minutes, or until set before cutting into 12 squares.

ASIA PACIFIC

Five Spice Chocolate Truffles

PREPARATION TIME: 20 minutes, plus infusing and chilling
COOKING TIME: 5 minutes

CHINA

MAKES: 30 truffles

100ml/3½fl oz/scant
   ½ cup double (heavy)
   cream
1 tbsp Chinese five spice
   powder
200g/7oz dark
   (bittersweet) chocolate,
   roughly chopped
2 tbsp unsweetened
   cocoa powder, sifted

1 Heat the cream with the five spice powder in a small saucepan over a low heat until it just begins to simmer. Remove from the heat and leave for 15 minutes for the flavour to infuse.

2 Pass the cream through a sieve into a clean saucepan and add the chocolate. Cook over a low heat, stirring frequently, until the chocolate is melted and the mixture is smooth. Pour into a heatproof bowl and leave to cool completely, then refrigerate for approximately 30 minutes until firm.

3 Roll teaspoonfuls of the mixture into balls and toss in the coca powder to coat. Place on a baking tray lined with baking paper and refrigerate for 30 minutes, or until firm.

ASIA
PACIFIC

Simple Chocolate & Raspberry Jam Cake

PREPARATION TIME: 20 minutes
COOKING TIME: 50–55 minutes

MAKES: 1 x 23cm/
9in cake

175g/6oz/¾ cup butter,
  plus extra for greasing
2 tbsp raspberry jam
250g/9oz/1¼ cups
  caster (granulated) sugar
3 eggs, lightly beaten
250g/9oz/2 cups self-
  raising flour
150g/5½oz/1 cup plus
  2 tbsp drinking chocolate
100ml/3½fl oz/scant ½
  cup milk
½ recipe quantity Creamy
  Chocolate Frosting
  (see page 28)

1 Preheat the oven to 180°C/350°F/gas 4. Grease a 23cm/9in spring-form cake pan with butter and line the base with baking paper.

2 In a small saucepan, melt the butter and jam together over a low heat and set aside to cool.

3 In a large bowl, beat the sugar and eggs together until thick and pale using an electric hand mixer. In a clean bowl, mix together the flour and drinking chocolate using a wooden spoon. Fold into the egg mixture with the melted butter and jam and the milk. Pour into the prepared pan.

4 Bake in the hot oven for 45–50 minutes until the cake is browned and just firm to the touch. Remove from the oven and leave the cake in the pan to cool for 10 minutes, then turn out on to a wire (cooling) rack to cool completely.

500ml/8¾fl oz/2 cups
  whipped cream
20g/¾oz milk chocolate,
  grated, to garnish

5 When cool slice the cake into 2 layers and use a palette knife to spread over the creamy chocolate frosting. Top with the whipped cream and decorate with a little extra chocolate frosting and grated chocolate.

ASIA
PACIFIC

Chocolate Anzac Biscuits

PREPARATION TIME: 420 minutes
COOKING TIME: 20–23 minutes

MAKES: 20 biscuits

75g/2¾oz/5 tbsp butter,
   chopped, plus extra for
   greasing
2 tbsp clear honey
½ tsp bicarbonate of soda
   (baking soda)
50g/1¾oz/½ cup
   rolled oats
75g/2¾oz/½ cup plus
   1 tbsp plain (all-purpose)
   flour
100g/3½oz/½ cup
   caster (granulated) sugar
3 tbsp desiccated (dried
   shredded) coconut
50g/1¾oz milk or dark
   (bittersweet) chocolate
   chips

1 Preheat the oven to 170°C/325°F/gas 3. Grease 2 large baking trays with butter.

2 In a small saucepan, heat the butter and honey over a low heat until just melted, then add the bicarbonate of soda. The mixture should fizz up for a moment or two, and then settle down. Remove from the heat and set aside to cool.

3 In a large bowl, combine all the remaining ingredients using a wooden spoon, then pour over the cooled mixture and mix together. Place 20 large teaspoonfuls of the mixture on the prepared baking trays, leaving approximately 10cm/4in between them to allow for spreading.

4 Bake in the hot oven for 15–18 minutes (the biscuits will still look soft). You may need to cook them in batches. Remove the biscuits from the oven and leave to cool on the trays for 5 minutes, then transfer to a wire (cooling) rack to cool completely.

Matcha Green Tea Crêpe Cake

PREPARATION TIME: 40 minutes, plus standing and chilling
COOKING TIME: 30 minutes

JAPAN

MAKES: 1 x 20cm
/ 8in cake

FOR THE CRÊPES
3 eggs
1 tsp vanilla extract
60g/2¼oz/⅓ cup caster
  (granulated) sugar
400ml/14fl oz/1⅔ cups
  milk, plus extra if needed
3 tbsp vegetable oil
250g/9oz/2 cups plain
  (all-purpose) flour
½ tsp salt
1 tbsp matcha powder
melted butter, for greasing

1 For the crêpes, whisk together the eggs, vanilla extract, sugar, milk and oil until combined. In a large bowl, combine the flour, salt and matcha powder. Make a well in the middle of the flour mixture and pour in half the liquid mixture. Mix well with a wooden spoon, adding the remaining liquid as required so that the batter resembles thin cream. Allow the batter to stand for 30 minutes before using, and add a little extra milk if required if it has thickened too much while standing – it should be the consistency of thin cream.

2 Heat a 20cm/8in non-stick crêpe pan over a low heat and brush with a little melted butter. Pour in just enough batter to coat the base of the pan, then swirl it around and pour off any excess. Leave the batter to cook until the edges of the crêpe dry and begin to lift (approximately 1 minute), then turn the crêpe over using a metal spatula. Cook for 30 seconds more, then remove from the pan and repeat until all of the crêpe batter has been used

FOR THE FILLING

1 tbsp unsweetened cocoa
  powder
400ml/14fl oz/1²⁄₃ cups
  double (heavy) cream
90g/3¼oz dark
  (bittersweet) chocolate,
  melted and cooled, plus
  15g/½oz, grated

– you should be able to make about 18 crêpes.
Cover the crêpes with cling film (plastic wrap) and
leave to cool completely.

3 For the filling, put the cocoa powder in a small
bowl and mix with 1 tbsp hot water, stirring until
smooth, then leave to cool. Put the cream and the
cooled cocoa mixture in a large bowl and beat
with an electric hand mixer just until soft peaks
form. Fold in the cooled melted chocolate, taking
care not to overmix.

4 Using a kitchen plate (around 19cm/7½in
diameter) as a template, cut around each crêpe
to form a neat circle. Place a crêpe on a serving
dish and spread evenly with a small amount of the
chocolate cream. Repeat this until all of the crêpes
have been stacked, using all but 2 tbsp of the
chocolate cream. Spread the reserved chocolate
cream thinly over the sides and top of the cake
with a palette knife.

5 Sprinkle over the grated chocolate and
refrigerate for 1 hour before serving.

ASIA
PACIFIC

Chocolate Chai Cookies

PREPARATION TIME: 20 minutes
COOKING TIME: 12–15 minutes

INDIA

MAKES: 24 cookies

125g/4½oz/½ cup butter,
   softened, plus extra for
   greasing
100g/3½oz/½ cup caster
   (granulated) sugar
100g/3½oz/½ cup soft
   brown sugar
1 tsp vanilla extract
1 egg, lightly beaten
100g/3½oz/1 cup
   rolled oats
125g/4½oz/1 cup
   self-raising flour
2 tbsp cocoa powder
50g/1¾oz/½ cup ground
   almonds
1 tsp ground cinnamon
1 tsp ground cardamom
½ tsp ground star anise
½ tsp ground ginger

1 Preheat the oven to 180°C/350°F/gas 4. Grease 2 large baking trays with butter.

2 In a large bowl, beat the butter and both sugars together until light and creamy using an electric hand mixer, then beat in the vanilla extract and egg. Stir in all the remaining ingredients until just combined. Place tablespoonfuls of the mixture on to the prepared baking trays, leaving approximately 5cm/2in of space between them to allow for spreading.

3 Bake in the hot oven for 12–15 minutes, or until the cookies are golden brown. (You may need to cook them in batches.) Remove the cookies from the oven and transfer them to a wire (cooling) rack to cool completely.

Chocolate Peppermint Slices

PREPARATION TIME: 30 minutes, plus chilling
COOKING TIME: 17–20 minutes

AUSTRALIA

MAKES: 24 squares

25g/1oz/2 tbsp butter,
  melted, plus extra for
  greasing
100g/3½oz/¾ cup
  self-raising flour
2 tbsp unsweetened cocoa
  powder
¼ tsp bicarbonate of soda
  (baking soda)
65g/2¼oz/5 tbsp caster
  (granulated) sugar
1 egg, lightly beaten

FOR THE FILLING

300g/10½oz/2
  cups plus 2 tbsp icing
  (confectioners') sugar
1 tbsp vegetable oil
1 tsp peppermint extract
2 tbsp milk (approximately)

1 Preheat the oven to 180°C/350°F/gas 4. Grease a shallow 23cm/9in square cake pan with butter and line with baking paper.

2 In a large bowl, mix the butter, flour, cocoa, bicarbonate of soda, sugar and 5 tbsp water together until smooth using a wooden spoon. Add the egg and mix until well combined. Pour into the prepared pan.

3 Bake in the hot oven for 12–15 minutes, or until the slice is just firm. Remove from the oven and leave the slice to cool completely in the pan.

4 For the filling, sift the icing sugar into a bowl. Add the vegetable oil, peppermint and 4 tbsp hot water and mix together until smooth, adding as much of the milk as is necessary for a soft consistency. Spread the filling evenly over the cake base, using a palette knife. Refrigerate the slice for 1 hour until firm.

FOR THE TOPPING

125g/4½oz dark
  (bittersweet) chocolate,
  broken into pieces
100g/3½oz/7 tbsp
  butter, chopped

5 For the topping, heat the chocolate and butter together in a small saucepan over a low heat until the chocolate has just melted, then stir until smooth using a wooden spoon. Spread the topping evenly over the filling, then refrigerate the slice for 1 hour.

6 Remove from the refrigerator and cut into 24 squares.

ASIA
PACIFIC

Chocolate Ice Cream & Ginger Biscuit Sandwiches

PREPARATION TIME: 30 minutes, plus chilling
COOKING TIME: 12–15 minutes

MAKES: 4 sandwiches

100g/3½oz/7 tbsp
  butter, softened, plus
  extra for greasing
100g/3½oz/¾ cup icing
  (confectioners') sugar
2 egg yolks
150g/5½oz/1 cup plus
  2 tbsp plain (all-purpose)
  flour, plus extra for
  dusting
4 tsp ground ginger
8 scoops Rich Chocolate
  Ice Cream (see page 30)
85g/3 oz/½ cup milk
  chocolate chips

1 In a bowl, beat the butter and sugar together until pale and light using an electric hand mixer, then beat in the egg yolks. In a clean bowl, mix the flour and ginger together, then gently stir into the butter mixture to form a dough. Wrap in cling film (plastic wrap), flatten and refrigerate for 45 minutes, or until the dough is firm but not hard.

2 Preheat the oven to 180°C/350°F/gas 4. Grease a baking tray with butter.

3 Roll the dough out on a lightly floured surface to 5mm/¼in thick, then cut out 8 evenly-sized biscuits. Place the biscuits on the baking tray, prick them with a fork and bake for 12–15 minutes, or until the biscuits are firm and lightly golden.

4 Remove from the oven and leave the biscuits on the tray to cool completely. Soften the

chocolate ice cream slightly and fold in the chocolate chips. Sandwich pairs of biscuits together with 1 scoop of chocolate ice cream in the middle of each.

Chocolate Melting Moments

PREPARATION TIME: 20 minutes
COOKING TIME: 8–10 minutes

AUSTRALIA / NZ

MAKES: 20 biscuits

125g/4½oz/½ cup
  butter, softened, plus
  extra for greasing
40g/1½oz/¼ cup icing
  (confectioners') sugar
125g/4½oz/1 cup plain
  (all-purpose) flour
3 tbsp unsweetened cocoa
  powder

1 Preheat the oven to 180°C/350°F/gas 4. Grease 2 large baking trays with butter.

2 In a large bowl, mix the butter and sugar together using a wooden spoon until light and fluffy. In a separate bowl, combine the flour and cocoa, then stir into the butter mixture until just combined (the mixture will be soft).

3 Place a little flour on your hands and roll the mixture into 20 balls. Place 10 balls on each baking tray, leaving around 5cm/2in between them to allow for spreading, then press the top of each biscuit down with a lightly floured fork.

4 Bake in the hot oven for 8–10 minutes, or until the biscuits are firm. Remove the melting moments from the oven and leave to cool on the baking trays for 5 minutes before transferring to a wire (cooling) rack to cool completely.

Chocolate & Banana Fritters

PREPARATION TIME: 20 minutes
COOKING TIME: 20–28 minutes

SERVES 4

200g/7oz/1½ cups
  self-raising flour
2 tbsp unsweetened
  cocoa powder
45g/1½oz/scant ¼
  cup caster sugar, plus
  extra for sprinkling
1 egg
250ml/9fl oz/1 cup milk
vegetable oil, for deep-
  frying
4 ripe, firm bananas,
  peeled and cut into thirds
1 recipe quantity Rich
  Chocolate Sauce
  (see page 25), to serve

1 In a large bowl, sift the flour and cocoa together, then add the sugar. In a clean bowl, whisk the egg and milk together using a hand whisk, then add to the flour mixture, stirring well with a wooden spoon to form a smooth batter.

2 Heat the oil in a wide frying pan until a cube of bread turns brown within 30 seconds of being placed in it. Dip the bananas into the batter, then deep-fry in batches of 3 pieces for 5–7 minutes until golden brown. Remove the bananas from the pan, drain on paper towels and sprinkle with a little extra sugar.

3 Serve the banana fritters immediately with the chocolate sauce.

ASIA
PACIFIC

Chocolate Pavlova

PREPARATION TIME: 20 minutes, plus cooling
COOKING TIME: 1 hour 10 minutes

AUSTRALIA/NZ

SERVES 4–6

4 egg whites
250g/9oz/1¼ cups
  caster (superfine) sugar
2 tsp cornflour (cornstarch)
1 tsp white wine vinegar
50g/1¾oz dark
  (bittersweet) chocolate,
  grated, plus extra for
  serving
250ml/9fl oz/1 cup
  double (heavy) cream
2 tbsp icing (confectioners')
  sugar
50g/1¾oz dark
  (bittersweet) or milk
  chocolate, melted

1 Preheat the oven to 170°C/325°F/gas 3. Draw a 23cm/9in circle on a sheet of baking paper, turn it over and place on a baking tray.

2 In a bowl, whisk the egg whites until stiff peaks form using an electric hand mixer, then gradually whisk in the sugar until the mixture is thick and shiny. Add the cornflour, vinegar and grated chocolate and whisk until just combined. Spoon on to the baking paper and spread over the circle.

3 Bake in the oven for 10 minutes. Turn the oven down to 140°C/275°F/gas 1 and bake for 1 hour. Turn the oven off but leave the pavlova inside.

4 In a bowl, whip the cream and icing sugar together to form soft peaks using an electric hand mixer. Once cooled, remove the pavlova from the oven and transfer to a plate. Top with the melted chocolate, the cream and the grated chocolate.

VARIATION
For added chocolate content,
you can replace the cream
with Chocolate Chantilly
Cream (see page 19).

Chocolate Lamingtons

PREPARATION TIME: 40 minutes, plus setting
COOKING TIME: 15–20 minutes

AUSTRALIA / NZ

MAKES: 16 lamingtons

25g/1oz/2 tbsp butter,
  melted, plus extra for
  greasing
4 eggs
100g/3½oz/½ cup
  caster (granulated) sugar
100g/3½oz/¾ cup
  self-raising flour
1 tbsp cornflour
  (cornstarch)

1 Preheat the oven to 180°C/350°F/gas 4. Grease a shallow 23cm/9in square cake pan with butter and line the base with baking paper.

2 In a large bowl, beat the eggs and sugar together using an electric hand mixer until thick and pale (around 5–10 minutes). In a separate bowl, combine the flour and cornflour, then fold into the egg mixture with the melted butter using a metal spoon until just mixed. Pour into the prepared pan.

3 Bake in the hot oven for 15–20 minutes until the cake is firm and lightly golden. Remove from the oven and leave the cake in the pan to cool for 10 minutes, then turn out on to a wire (cooling) rack to cool completely. With a sharp knife, cut the cooled cake into 16 squares, removing the crusts.

EVERYBODY LOVES CHOCOLATE

FOR THE COATING
500g/1lb 2oz/4 cups
  icing (confectioners')
  sugar, sifted
3 tbsp unsweetened cocoa
  powder, sifted
25g/1oz/2 tbsp butter,
  melted
125ml/4fl oz/½ cup milk
175g/6oz/2 cups
  desiccated (dried
  shredded) coconut

4 For the coating, combine the icing sugar and cocoa in a large bowl. Using a wooden spoon, stir in the melted butter, milk and as much of 125ml/4fl oz/½ cup hot water as is needed to make the mixture the consistency of thick cream. Dip each piece of cake into the coating until it is well covered, then toss the coated cake in the coconut until completely covered. Leave to set on a wire (cooling) rack.

**ASIA
PACIFIC**

Spiced Hot Chocolates

PREPARATION TIME: 10 minutes, plus standing
COOKING TIME: 15 minutes

SERVES 4

1l/35fl oz/4¼ cups milk

50g/1¾oz/¼ cup soft
  brown sugar

6 green cardamom pods,
  crushed

6 cloves

1 cinnamon stick

1 star anise, lightly crushed

½ tsp whole coriander
  seeds, lightly crushed

½ tsp ground nutmeg

¼ tsp dried chilli (hot
  pepper) flakes

3 tbsp unsweetened
  cocoa powder

½ tsp vanilla extract

4 tbsp softly whipped
  cream

2 tbsp grated chocolate,
  to serve

1 In a medium-size saucepan, combine the milk, sugar, cardamom, cloves, cinnamon, star anise, coriander seeds, nutmeg and dried chilli flakes and cook over a medium heat until hot. Remove the pan from the heat, whisk in the cocoa using a hand whisk, then leave to stand for 20 minutes.

2 Strain the spiced milk into a clean saucepan and reheat until just boiling. Add the vanilla extract, then divide the chocolate drink equally between 4 cups or heatproof glasses. Add a spoonful of softly whipped cream and a sprinkle of grated chocolate to serve.

EUROPE

Chocolate Éclairs

PREPARATION TIME: 40 minutes, plus chilling
COOKING TIME: 20–25 minutes

FRANCE

MAKES: 6 large éclairs

1 recipe quantity Choux
　Pastry (see page 20)
250ml/9fl oz/1 cup
　double (heavy) cream,
　whipped to soft peaks
1 recipe quantity Dark
　Chocolate Ganache
　(see page 27)
2 tbsp finely chopped
　pistachio nuts, to garnish
　(optional)

1 Preheat the oven to 220°C/425°F/gas 7. Line a baking tray with baking paper. Spoon the choux pastry into a piping bag with a plain 1cm/½in nozzle and pipe 6 x 13cm/5in pastry lengths on the lined baking tray. Sprinkle lightly with water.

2 Bake in the hot oven for 20–25 minutes, or until golden brown. Ensure the middles are dry.

3 Remove the éclairs from the oven and transfer to a wire (cooling) rack. Pierce the sides with a knife so the steam can escape. Leave to cool, then split lengthways and scrape out any wet dough left.

4 Using a clean piping bag with a fluted 1cm/½in nozzle, pipe the whipped cream into the middle of each éclair. Using a palette knife, smooth the dark chocolate ganache along the top of each éclair. Sprinkle over the chopped pistachios, if using, and refrigerate for 30 minutes before serving.

Profiteroles with Coffee Cream & Chocolate Sauce

PREPARATION TIME: 40 minutes
COOKING TIME: 20–25 minutes

MAKES: 12 profiteroles

1 recipe quantity Choux
  Pastry (see page 20)
250ml/9fl oz/1 cup
  double (heavy) cream
2 tsp instant coffee
  granules, dissolved
  in ½ tsp warm water
  and cooled
1 tbsp coffee liqueur
2 tbsp icing (confectioners')
  sugar, sifted
1 recipe quantity Rich
  Chocolate Sauce
  (see page 25), to serve

1 Preheat the oven to 220°C/425°F/gas 7. Line a large baking tray with baking paper. Spoon 12 tablespoonfuls of the choux pastry on to the lined baking tray. Sprinkle lightly with water.

2 Bake in the hot oven for 20–25 minutes, or until golden brown. Ensure the middles are dry.

3 Remove the profiteroles from the oven and transfer to a wire (cooling) rack. Pierce each profiterole with a knife so the steam can escape. Leave to cool, then split in half and scrape out any wet dough left.

4 For the filling, put the cream, coffee, liqueur and sugar in a bowl and whip to soft peaks using an electric hand mixer. Spoon or pipe this filling into the profiteroles. Serve your profiteroles drizzled with the chocolate sauce.

Strawberry & Chocolate Mille-feuilles

PREPARATION TIME: 45 minutes, plus cooling
COOKING TIME: 20–25 minutes

SERVES 4

375g/13oz ready-rolled
  puff pastry
plain (all-purpose) flour,
  for dusting
2 tbsp milk
4 tsp caster (superfine)
  sugar
250ml/9fl oz/1 cup
  double (heavy) cream,
  whipped to soft peaks
150g/5½oz/1 cup
  strawberries, hulled
  and thinly sliced
100g/3½oz dark
  (bittersweet) or milk
  chocolate, melted and
  left to cool

1 Preheat the oven to 190°C/375°F/gas 5. Unroll the pastry on a lightly floured surface and cut it into 8 rectangles, around 10 x 7cm/4 x 2¾in. Place the rectangles on a baking tray and lightly brush the tops with the milk. Using a fork, prick the pastry in 5 or 6 places, then sprinkle with the caster sugar.

2 Bake in the hot oven for 20–25 minutes, or until the pastry has risen and is golden brown. Remove from the oven and leave on the baking tray to cool.

3 To assemble the mille-feuilles, place a rectangle on each plate and spread over a spoonful of whipped cream. Top evenly with the strawberries and drizzle over the melted chocolate. Repeat with a second set of layers – pastry, cream, strawberries and chocolate – and serve immediately.

EUROPE

Chocolate & Pistachio Biscotti

PREPARATION TIME: 35 minutes
COOKING TIME: 50–65 minutes

ITALY

MAKES: around
20 biscotti

125g/4½oz/½ cup plus
  2 tbsp caster (granulated)
  sugar
1 egg
125g/4½oz/1 cup plain
  (all-purpose) flour, plus
  extra for dusting
2 tbsp unsweetened cocoa
  powder
½ tsp baking powder
50g/1¾oz/¾ cup shelled
  pistachio nuts, roughly
  chopped

1 Preheat the oven to 170°C/325°F/gas 3. Line a large baking tray with baking paper.

2 In a bowl, beat the sugar and egg together until thick using an electric hand mixer. In a separate bowl, combine all the remaining ingredients using a metal spoon and fold into the egg mixture to form a dough. Gently knead the dough on a lightly floured surface for around 30 seconds. Form a log (about 18 x 5cm/7 x 2in) and place on the tray.

3 Bake in the hot oven for 20–25 minutes, or until firm. Remove from the oven, turning the temperature down to 140°C/275°F/gas 1, and leave to cool. When the dough is cold, cut it into 20 slices, each around 5mm/¼in thick, using a serrated knife.

4 Place the slices on a fresh lined baking tray and bake them in the warm oven for 30–40 minutes, turning once, until they are dry. Remove from the oven and leave to cool.

Chocolate Macaroons

PREPARATION TIME: 20 minutes
COOKING TIME: 10–15 minutes

FRANCE

MAKES: 24 macaroons

3 egg whites
200g/7oz/1 cup caster (superfine) sugar
1½ tbsp plain (all-purpose) flour
2 tbsp unsweetened cocoa powder
150g/5½oz/1½ cups ground almonds

1 Preheat the oven to 180°C/350°F/gas 4. Line 2 large baking trays with baking paper.

2 In a clean bowl, whisk the egg whites to soft peaks using an electric hand mixer. Gradually add the sugar and continue to whisk until stiff and the sugar has dissolved (around 5 minutes). In a separate bowl, combine the flour, cocoa and ground almonds using a wooden spoon, then gently fold into the egg whites until just combined. Place 24 tablespoonfuls of the mixture on the prepared baking trays, leaving approximately 5cm/2in between them to allow for spreading.

3 Bake in the warm oven for 10–15 minutes, or until the macaroons are dry on the outside but still moist in the middle. (You may need to cook them in batches.) Remove the macaroons from the oven and leave on the baking trays to cool completely.

EUROPE

Hazelnut Thumbprints

PREPARATION TIME: 25 minutes
COOKING TIME: 10–12 minutes

MAKES: 24 biscuits

125g/4½oz/½ cup
  butter, softened, plus
  extra for greasing
125g/4½oz/½ cup plus
  2 tbsp caster (granulated)
  sugar
1 egg, lightly beaten
75g/2¾oz/½ cup plus
  1 tbsp plain (all-purpose)
  flour
75g/2¾oz/½ cup plus
  1 tbsp self-raising flour
2 tbsp unsweetened cocoa
  powder
150g/5½oz/⅔ cup
  chocolate hazelnut
  spread
icing (confectioners') sugar,
  sifted, for dusting

1 Preheat the oven to 180°C/350°F/gas 4. Grease 2 large baking trays with butter.

2 In a large bowl, beat the butter and sugar together until pale and creamy using an electric hand mixer, then beat in the egg, beating well to combine. In a separate bowl, mix together both flours and the cocoa using a wooden spoon, then stir into the butter mixture to form a dough.

3 Roll into 24 balls the size of walnuts and place on the trays, leaving around 5cm/2in between them. Push the middle of each ball down with your thumb to create an indent, then place a teaspoonful of the chocolate hazelnut spread into each hole.

4 Bake in the hot oven for 10–12 minutes, or until firm. (You may need to cook them in batches.) Remove from the oven and leave to cool on the trays for 10 minutes before transferring to a wire (cooling) rack to cool completely. Dust with icing sugar.

Chocolate Madeleines

PREPARATION TIME: 15 minutes
COOKING TIME: 15–17 minutes

FRANCE

MAKES: 12 madeleines

100g/3½oz/7 tbsp
  butter, chopped, plus
  extra for greasing
75g/2¾oz dark
  (bittersweet) chocolate,
  broken into pieces
75g/2¾oz/½ cup plus
  1 tbsp plain (all-purpose)
  flour
½ tsp baking powder
pinch salt
2 eggs
100g/3½oz/½ cup
  caster (granulated) sugar
icing (confectioners') sugar,
  sifted, for dusting

1 Preheat the oven to 180°C/350°F/gas 4. Grease a 12-hole madeleine pan with butter.

2 In a saucepan, heat the butter and chocolate over a low heat until melted, then set aside to cool.

3 Sift the flour and baking powder into a bowl and add the salt. In a separate bowl, beat the eggs and sugar together until the mixture is light in colour using an electric hand mixer, then whisk in the chocolate mixture. Using a metal spoon, gently fold in the flour mix. Divide the mixture between the 12 holes in the pan, but don't overfill!

4 Bake in the hot oven for 10–12 minutes until the cakes are firm to the touch. Remove from the oven and leave the madeleines in the pan to cool for 10 minutes, then turn out on to a wire (cooling) rack to cool completely. Dust with icing sugar.

EUROPE

Chocolate Caramel Tartlets

PREPARATION TIME: 35 minutes, plus setting
COOKING TIME: 15 minutes

FRANCE

**MAKES: 4 x 10cm/
4in tartlets**

400g/14oz/2 cups
  granulated sugar
125g/4½oz/½ cup
  butter, chopped
125ml/4fl oz/½ cup
  double (heavy) cream
4 x 10cm/4in Sweet
  Shortcrust Pastry cases,
  baked (see pages 22–3)
½ recipe quantity Dark
  Chocolate Ganache
  (see page 27)
4 tbsp grated or roughly
  chopped chocolate,
  to serve
1 tbsp unsweetened cocoa
  powder, sifted, for dusting

1 In a medium-size saucepan, mix 125ml/4fl oz/½ cup water and the sugar together over a low heat, then stir with a metal spoon from time to time until the sugar has dissolved completely. Turn up the heat and boil vigorously for 10–12 minutes until the mixture forms a dark caramel, swirling the pan from time to time. Remove from the heat, add the butter and cream (being careful as the mixture will hiss and spit) and stir well until combined using a wooden spoon. Set the caramel mixture aside to cool for 15 minutes, then divide it equally between the baked pastry cases and leave to set for 15–20 minutes.

2 Top each tartlet with dark chocolate ganache, spreading it over the caramel evenly with a palette knife. Leave the tartlets to set at room temperature for 1–2 hours. Decorate the tarts with chopped or grated chocolate and a little sifted cocoa powder just before serving.

Chocolate-almond Friands with Raspberries

PREPARATION TIME: 15 minutes
COOKING TIME: 12–15 minutes

FRANCE

MAKES: 24 friands

100g/3½oz/7 tbsp
  butter, melted, plus extra
  for greasing
90g/3¼oz/heaped
  ¾ cup plus 1 tbsp
  ground almonds
225g/8oz/1⅔ cups icing
  (confectioners') sugar
70g/2½oz/½ cup plus
  1 tbsp plain (all-purpose)
  flour
2 tbsp unsweetened cocoa
  powder
6 egg whites
1 tsp vanilla extract
24 raspberries

1 Preheat the oven to 180°C/350°F/gas 4. Grease 24 friand moulds or 2 x 12-hole mini-muffin tins with butter.

2 In a large bowl, mix the melted butter, ground almonds, sugar, flour, cocoa, egg whites and vanilla extract together until combined using a wooden spoon. Divide the mixture between the prepared moulds or holes in the tins, taking care not to overfill, then place a raspberry on top of each friand.

3 Bake in the hot oven for 12–15 minutes until the friands are lightly browned. Remove from the oven and leave the friands in the moulds to cool for 5 minutes, then turn them out on to a wire (cooling) rack to cool completely.

Chocolate-dipped Shortbreads

PREPARATION TIME: 20 minutes, plus setting
COOKING TIME: 10–12 minutes

SCOTLAND

MAKES: 18 shortbreads

125g/4½oz/½ cup
  butter, softened
75g/2¾oz/½ cup plus
  ½ tbsp icing
  (confectioners') sugar
125g/4½oz/1 cup plain
  (all-purpose) flour
100g/3½oz dark
  (bittersweet) chocolate,
  melted and left to cool

1 Preheat the oven to 180°C/350°F/gas 4. Line a large baking tray with baking paper.

2 In a large bowl, mix together the butter, sugar and flour until well combined using a wooden spoon. Roll 18 teaspoonfuls of the mixture into balls and place on the prepared baking tray, flattening them slightly, leaving approximately 10cm/4in between them to allow for spreading.

3 Bake in the hot oven for 10–12 minutes, or until the shortbreads are lightly browned. Remove from the oven and transfer the shortbreads to a wire (cooling) rack to cool completely.

4 Half-dip the cooled shortbreads into the melted chocolate and leave on a clean sheet of baking paper to set.

EUROPE

Chocolate Meringues with Blackberries

PREPARATION TIME: 20 minutes, plus cooling
COOKING TIME: 40 minutes

FRANCE

MAKES: 8–10
meringues

3 egg whites
150g/5½oz/¾ cup
   caster (superfine) sugar
50g/1¾oz dark
   (bittersweet) chocolate,
   grated, plus 50g/1¾oz
   melted and left to cool
1 tsp unsweetened cocoa
   powder
1 recipe quantity
   Chocolate Chantilly
   Cream (see page 19)
185g/6½oz/1½ cups
   blackberries, to serve
icing (confectioners') sugar,
   sifted, for dusting

1 Preheat the oven to 140°C/275°F/gas 1. Line 2 baking trays with baking paper.

2 In a bowl, whisk the egg whites until stiff peaks form using an electric hand mixer, then gradually whisk in the sugar until the mixture is thick and shiny and the sugar has dissolved. Gently fold in the grated chocolate and cocoa using a metal spoon. Place 16–20 heaped tablespoonfuls of the mixture on the lined baking trays.

3 Bake in the warm oven for 40 minutes, then turn the oven off but leave the meringues inside to cool.

4 Remove the meringues from the oven and sandwich them together in pairs with the chocolate chantilly cream. Drizzle over the melted chocolate. Serve with blackberries, dusted with icing sugar.

EUROPE

Cranberry & White Chocolate Scones

PREPARATION TIME: 20 minutes
COOKING TIME: 15–20 minutes

MAKES: 6 large scones

75g/2¾oz/5 tbsp butter,
   chilled and chopped, plus
   extra for greasing and
   to serve
250g/9oz/2 cups self-
   raising flour, plus extra
   for dusting
45g/1½oz/scant ¼ cup
   caster (granulated) sugar
75g/2¾oz white
   chocolate chips
100g/3½oz/¾ cup plus
   1 tbsp dried cranberries
6 tbsp milk, plus extra for
   brushing
1 egg, lightly beaten

1 Preheat the oven to 190°C/375°F/gas 5. Grease a large baking tray with butter.

2 Place the flour and sugar in a large bowl and lightly rub in the butter with your fingertips until it resembles breadcrumbs. Stir in the chocolate chips and cranberries using a wooden spoon. In a small bowl, beat together the milk and egg. Add this to the flour mixture until it forms a soft dough.

3 Turn the dough out on to a lightly floured board and pat it out until it is around 2.5cm/1in thick. Cut out 6 circles using a scone cutter and place on the tray. Brush the tops with a little extra milk.

4 Bake in the hot oven for 15–20 minutes, or until golden brown. Remove from the oven and transfer to a wire (cooling) rack to cool, then transfer to a serving plate and serve warm or cold with butter.

Fig & Chocolate Bread Pudding

PREPARATION TIME: 20 minutes, plus standing
COOKING TIME: 35–40 minutes

SERVES 4–6

25g/1oz/2 tbsp butter,
   softened, plus extra
   for greasing
1 small brioche loaf,
   cut into 8 slices
100g/3½oz soft dried
   figs, sliced
100g/3½oz dark
   (bittersweet) chocolate,
   grated
4 eggs
125g/4½oz/½ cup plus
   2 tbsp caster (granulated)
   sugar
250ml/9fl oz/1 cup milk
250ml/9fl oz/1 cup
   double (heavy) cream
1 tsp vanilla extract

1 Butter the brioche slices on one side and cut in half diagonally. Arrange half of the slices in the base of the prepared dish. Scatter over the figs and chocolate, then top with the remaining brioche slices.

2 Beat all the remaining ingredients together in a bowl using a hand whisk, then pour the resulting batter through a sieve over the top of the brioche slices. Leave to stand for 30 minutes.

3 Preheat the oven to 150°C/300°F/gas 2. Grease a 1.5-l/52-fl oz/6½-cup capacity ovenproof dish with butter.

4 Place the ovenproof dish in a bain-marie (see page 13) and bake in the warm oven for 35–40 minutes, or until the pudding is just firm around the edges but still slightly wobbly in the middle. Remove from the oven and serve immediately.

Dark Chocolate Orange Bavarois

PREPARATION TIME: 25 minutes, plus cooling and chilling
COOKING TIME: 5 minutes

SERVES 4

200ml/7fl oz/scant
  1 cup milk
125g/4½oz dark
  (bittersweet) chocolate,
  broken into pieces
2 tbsp orange liqueur
3 sheets leaf gelatine
finely grated zest of
  1 orange
375ml/13fl oz/1½ cups
  double (heavy) cream,
  whipped to soft peaks
orange slices, to decorate

1 In a medium-size saucepan, heat the milk, chocolate and orange liqueur together over a low heat until the chocolate melts. Remove from the heat and stir until smooth using a wooden spoon.

2 Meanwhile, soak the gelatine sheets in a bowl of cold water for 5–10 minutes until soft, then remove them, wring out any excess water and stir into the chocolate mixture until they dissolve. Pour into a clean bowl and set aside for approximately 1 hour until cool and beginning to thicken.

3 Fold in the orange zest and two-thirds of the whipped cream using a metal spoon, then divide the mixture equally between 4 dishes. Refrigerate for 3 hours or overnight. Top each dessert with a spoonful of the remaining whipped cream and decorate with orange slices just before serving.

Chocolate Florentines

PREPARATION TIME: 30 minutes, plus cooling and setting
COOKING TIME: 10–13 minutes

MAKES: 24 florentines

50g/1¾oz/3½ tbsp
   butter
45g/1½oz/scant ¼ cup
   caster (granulated) sugar
2 tsp clear honey
50g/1¾oz/½ cup flaked
   (sliced) almonds
50g/1¾oz/¼ cup red
   glacé cherries, chopped
50g/1¾oz/⅓ cup
   sultanas (golden raisins)
150g/5½oz milk
   chocolate, melted
   and cooled

1 Preheat the oven to 180°C/350°F/gas 4. Line 2 large baking trays with baking paper.

2 In a saucepan, melt the butter, sugar and honey together over a low heat. Remove from the heat.

3 In a bowl, mix together the almonds, glacé cherries and sultanas, then pour in the butter mixture, stirring with a wooden spoon to combine. Place tablespoonfuls of the mixture on the lined baking trays, leaving 5cm/2in between them, then press down lightly to flatten the mixture into rounds.

4 Bake in the oven for 6–8 minutes, or until golden. Remove from the oven, cool for 5 minutes, then transfer to a wire (cooling) rack to cool completely.

5 When cold, turn the biscuits over (the backs will be smooth), then spread with melted chocolate and make lines using a fork. Leave on the wire (cooling) rack until the chocolate is set.

140   **EVERYBODY LOVES CHOCOLATE**

White Chocolate & Raspberry Eton Mess

PREPARATION TIME: 10 minutes

SERVES 4

300ml/10½fl oz/1¼
  cups double (heavy)
  cream
1 tbsp caster (granulated)
  sugar
2 tbsp raspberry liqueur
8 crispy-style meringues
100g/3½oz white
  chocolate, melted and
  left to cool
125g/4½oz/1 cup
  raspberries, lightly
  crushed

1 In a large bowl, whip the cream, sugar and liqueur together until the mixture just forms soft peaks using an electric hand mixer.

2 Put the meringues in a plastic food bag, crush them lightly with a rolling pin, then tip them into the cream mixture and mix together using a wooden spoon. Fold in the melted chocolate and raspberries.

3 Spoon the mixture into 4 serving dishes and serve immediately.

EUROPE

White Chocolate Panna Cottas

PREPARATION TIME: 20 minutes, plus cooling and chilling
COOKING TIME: 5 minutes

ITALY

SERVES 4

3 sheets leaf gelatine
250ml/9fl oz/1 cup
  double (heavy) cream
125ml/4fl oz/½ cup milk
100g/3½oz white
  chocolate, broken into
  pieces
2 tbsp caster (granulated)
  sugar
1 tsp vanilla extract
125g/4½oz/1 cup
  raspberries, seeds
  removed
2 tbsp icing (confectioners')
  sugar, sifted

1 Soak the gelatine sheets in a bowl of cold water for 5–10 minutes until soft.

2 In a small saucepan, heat the cream, milk, chocolate, sugar and vanilla extract together over a low heat until the chocolate melts. Remove from the heat and stir with a wooden spoon until smooth. Remove the gelatine from the water and wring out any excess. Drop the gelatine into the cream mixture and stir briefly until dissolved.

3 Divide the mixture evenly between 4 x 125-ml/ 4-fl oz/½-cup capacity moulds on a tray and set aside to cool for around 30 minutes. Refrigerate the panna cottas for 3 hours or overnight.

4 In a blender, pulse the raspberries and icing sugar to a purée to make a coulis. Dip the moulds briefly into hot water and run a blunt/round-bladed knife around the sides. Turn the panna cottas out on to plates and serve with the coulis.

White Chocolate Crème Brûlées

PREPARATION TIME: 20 minutes, plus chilling
COOKING TIME: 45–50 minutes

FRANCE

SERVES 4

5 egg yolks
130g/4¾oz/⅔ cup caster
  (granulated) sugar
500ml/17fl oz/2 cups
  double (heavy) cream
125g/4½oz white
  chocolate, broken
  into pieces
½ tsp vanilla extract

1 Preheat the oven to 120°C/250°F/gas ½.

2 In a large bowl, beat the egg yolks and 100g/
3½oz/½ cup of the sugar together using a
hand whisk. In a saucepan, heat the cream and
chocolate over a low heat until the chocolate
melts. Remove from the heat and whisk until
smooth, then whisk it into the egg yolk mixture
with the vanilla extract until well combined.

3 Divide the mixture evenly between 4 x 150-ml/
5-fl oz/⅔-cup capacity ovenproof ramekins.
Place the ramekins in a bain-marie (see page 13)
and bake in the warm oven for 35–40 minutes,
or until the custards are just set.

4 Remove from the oven and take the ramekins
out of the bain-marie using tongs, then leave to
cool for 30 minutes before refrigerating overnight.

5 Remove from the refrigerator. Sprinkle the remaining sugar over the top of each dessert and place under a very hot grill (broiler) until the sugar melts and caramelizes (or use a domestic blowtorch). Serve immediately.

EUROPE

Black Cherry Trifle

PREPARATION TIME: 30 minutes, plus chilling
COOKING TIME: 50 minutes

SERVES 4–6

200g/7oz trifle sponges
   or plain cake, sliced
4 tbsp cherry brandy
400g/14oz/2 cups
   canned cherries, drained,
   syrup reserved
250ml/9fl oz/1 cup
   double (heavy) cream
2 tbsp caster (granulated)
   sugar
100g/3½oz dark
   (bittersweet) chocolate,
   melted and left to cool
6 ripe cherries, to decorate

1 Start by making the custard. In a small saucepan, heat the milk and cream over a low heat until just warm. In a large bowl, whisk the egg yolks, sugar and cocoa together using a hand whisk, then whisk in the warm milk mixture. Return the mixture to the pan with the vanilla extract and stir constantly with a wooden spoon until the mixture begins to thicken and coats the back of the spoon. Do not boil. Transfer to a heatproof bowl, cover with cling film (plastic wrap) and leave to cool.

2 Place the trifle sponges or sliced cake into the base of a large serving bowl and sprinkle over the cherry brandy. Scatter the canned cherries over the sponge base, along with 4 tbsp of the reserved cherry syrup, then top with the cold chocolate custard.

**FOR THE CREAMY
CHOCOLATE CUSTARD**
375ml/13fl oz/1½ cups
  milk
375ml/13fl oz/1½ cups
  double (heavy) cream
8 egg yolks
150g/5½oz/¾ cup
  caster (granulated) sugar
2 tbsp unsweetened cocoa
  powder
1 tsp vanilla extract

3 In a large bowl, whip the cream with the sugar until thick but not too stiff using an electric hand mixer, then spread it over the custard in the bowl. Drizzle over half of the melted chocolate. Refrigerate the trifle for 2 hours or overnight.

4 Meanwhile, half-dip the cherries in the remaining melted chocolate, leave them to set on baking paper and then use to decorate the trifle before serving.

EUROPE

Hot Chocolate Soufflés

PREPARATION TIME: 25 minutes
COOKING TIME: 20–23 minutes

FRANCE

SERVES 4

melted butter, for greasing
80g/3oz/⅓ cup plus
  1 tbsp caster (granulated)
  sugar, plus extra for
  coating
2 tbsp cornflour
  (cornstarch)
250ml/9fl oz/1 cup milk
100g/3½oz dark
  (bittersweet) chocolate,
  broken into pieces
3 eggs, separated, plus
  2 extra egg whites
icing (confectioners') sugar,
  sifted, for dusting

1 Preheat the oven to 190°C/375°F/gas 5. Grease 4 x 200ml/7fl oz/scant 1-cup capacity ovenproof cups with melted butter and coat lightly with caster sugar.

2 In a small bowl, mix the cornflour to a paste with 2 tbsp of the milk. In a medium-size saucepan, heat the remaining milk with the chocolate and half of the caster sugar over a low heat. When the chocolate has melted, whisk in the cornflour paste using a hand whisk. Continue whisking until the mixture boils and thickens, then turn down to a simmer and cook for 1 minute more. Remove from the heat and allow to cool for a few minutes before beating in the egg yolks. Cover with cling film (plastic wrap) and set the mixture aside to cool completely.

3 In a large bowl, whisk all the egg whites to soft peaks using an electric hand mixer, then add the remaining caster sugar and continue to whisk until

EVERYBODY LOVES CHOCOLATE

stiff but not dry. Gently fold the whisked whites into the chocolate mixture using a metal spoon, then divide equally between the prepared cups.

4 Bake in the hot oven for 15–18 minutes, or until the soufflés are well risen. Remove from the oven, dust with icing sugar and serve immediately.

Chocolate Bundt Cake

PREPARATION TIME: 20 minutes
COOKING TIME: 55–60 minutes

GERMANY

MAKES: 1 x 25cm/
10in cake

200g/7oz/¾ cup plus
   2 tbsp butter, softened, plus
   extra for greasing
400g/14oz/2 cups caster
   (granulated) sugar
3 eggs, lightly beaten
300g/10½oz/2½ cups self-
   raising flour
2 tbsp unsweetened cocoa
   powder, plus extra for dusting
150ml/5fl oz/⅔ cup milk
1 tsp vanilla extract
125g/4½oz dark (bittersweet)
   or milk chocolate chips
1 recipe quantity Shiny
   Chocolate Frosting
   (see page 29)
3–5 tbsp grated chocolate,
   to serve

1 Preheat the oven to 170°C/325°F/gas 3. Grease a 25cm/10in bundt pan with butter.

2 In a large bowl, beat the butter and sugar together until light and creamy using an electric hand mixer, then gradually whisk in the eggs. Fold in the flour, cocoa, milk, vanilla extract and chocolate chips until just combined using a metal spoon. Spoon into the prepared pan.

3 Bake in the hot oven for 55–60 minutes, or until a skewer inserted into the middle of the cake comes out clean. Remove from the oven and leave the cake in the pan to cool for 10 minutes.

4 Turn the cake out on to a wire (cooling) rack and, while still warm, dust over the cocoa powder, drizzle over the shiny chocolate frosting and add the grated chocolate.

Steamed Espresso Chocolate Pudding

PREPARATION TIME: 20 minutes
COOKING TIME: 1¾ hours

UNITED KINGDOM

SERVES 4–6

100g/3½oz/7 tbsp
   butter, softened, plus
   extra for greasing
100g/3½oz/½ cup
   caster (granulated) sugar
2 eggs, lightly beaten
100g/3½oz/¾ cup
   self-raising flour
2 tbsp unsweetened
   cocoa powder
100g/3½oz dark
   (bittersweet) chocolate,
   melted
2 tbsp milk

1 Grease a 1.25-l/440fl oz/5-cup capacity heatproof pudding basin with butter. In a large bowl, beat the butter and sugar together until light and creamy using an electric hand mixer, then add the eggs a little at a time until smooth. Sift the flour and cocoa together, then fold into the mixture with the melted chocolate and milk.

2 Spoon into the prepared basin and cover with a double layer of foil secured with string. Place the basin in a large saucepan and fill with water to come halfway up the side of the basin. Bring the water to the boil, turn down to a simmer and steam the pudding for 1¾ hours, adding extra boiling water to the pan as required.

FOR THE ESPRESSO CHOCOLATE SAUCE

250ml/9fl oz/1 cup double (heavy) cream
150g/5½oz dark (bittersweet) chocolate, broken into pieces
60ml/2fl oz/¼ cup hot, strong espresso coffee
1 tbsp coffee liqueur

3 While the pudding is steaming, make the sauce. In a small saucepan, combine the cream and chocolate over a low heat until the chocolate has just melted. Remove the pan from the heat and stir in the coffee and liqueur.

4 Remove the basin from the saucepan and leave to cool for 10 minutes, then turn the pudding out on to a serving plate. Serve with the espresso chocolate sauce.

EUROPE

Chocolate Polenta Cake

PREPARATION TIME: 20 minutes
COOKING TIME: 30–35 minutes

MAKES: 1 x 23cm/
9in cake

125g/4½oz/½ cup
  butter, softened, plus
  extra for greasing
250g/9oz dark
  (bittersweet) chocolate,
  broken into pieces
5 eggs, separated
150g/5½oz/¾ cup
  caster (granulated) sugar
4 tbsp dark rum
125g/4½oz/¾ cup
  plus 1 tbsp fine polenta
  (cornmeal)

1 Preheat the oven to 180°C/350°F/gas 4. Grease a 23cm/9in spring-form cake pan with butter and line the base with baking paper.

2 In a saucepan, combine the butter and chocolate over a low heat until the chocolate melts. Remove from the heat and set aside to cool.

3 In a bowl, beat the egg yolks and sugar together until pale and light using an electric hand mixer. Stir in the chocolate mixture using a wooden spoon.

4 In a clean bowl, whisk the egg whites until stiff, then fold into the chocolate base with the rum and polenta. Pour into the prepared pan.

5 Bake for 25–30 minutes, or until set but slightly wobbly in the middle. Remove from the oven and leave in the pan to cool for 15 minutes, then turn out on to a wire (cooling) rack to cool completely.

Chocolate Crêpes with Chestnut Cream

PREPARATION TIME: 25 minutes, plus standing
COOKING TIME: 20 minutes

SERVES 4

150g/5½oz/1 cup plus
  2 tbsp plain (all-purpose)
  flour
2 tbsp unsweetened cocoa
  powder, sifted
2 tsp caster (granulated)
  sugar
1 egg, lightly beaten
300ml/10½fl oz/
  1¼ cups milk
25g/1oz/2 tbsp butter,
  melted, plus extra for
  cooking the crêpes
icing (confectioners') sugar,
  sifted, for dusting

1 In a large bowl, combine the flour, cocoa and caster sugar, stirring with a wooden spoon. In a clean bowl, beat together the egg, milk and melted butter together using a hand whisk. Make a well in the middle of the flour mixture and pour in half the liquid mixture. Mix well with a wooden spoon, adding the remaining liquid as required so that the batter resembles thin cream. Allow the batter to stand for 30 minutes before using, and add a little extra milk if required if it has thickened too much while standing – it should be the consistency of thin cream.

2 While the batter is resting, make the filling. In a large bowl, beat the chestnut purée until smooth using an electric hand mixer. Stir in the cream, cinnamon and sugar, then set aside until needed.

FOR FILLING
AND TOPPING:

200g/7oz canned,
  unsweetened chestnut
  purée
250ml/9fl oz/1 cup
  double (heavy) cream
1 tsp ground cinnamon
2 tbsp caster (granulated)
  sugar
1 recipe quantity Double
  Chocolate Sauce
  (see page 24)

3 Heat a 20cm/8in non-stick crêpe pan over a low heat and brush with a little melted butter. Pour in just enough batter to coat the base of the pan, then swirl it around and pour off any excess. Leave the batter to cook until the edges of the crêpe dry and begin to lift (approximately 1 minute), then turn the crêpe over using a metal spatula. Cook for 30 seconds more, then remove from the pan and repeat until all of the crêpe batter has been used (you should make 12 crêpes in total).

4 Spread each warm crêpe with the chestnut cream and fold into quarters.

5 Place 3 chocolate crêpes on each plate, top with the double chocolate sauce and serve straight away.

EUROPE

Chocolate Tiramisu

PREPARATION TIME: 25 minutes, plus chilling

ITALY

SERVES 4–6

2 eggs, separated, plus
  3 extra egg yolks
100g/3½oz/½ cup
  caster (granulated) sugar
250g/9oz/1 cup
  mascarpone cheese,
  softened
100g/3½oz dark
  (bittersweet) chocolate,
  melted and cooled, plus
  4 tbsp grated
350ml/12fl oz/scant
  1½ cups strong coffee,
  cooled
4 tbsp Marsala wine
20 sponge-finger biscuits
2 tbsp unsweetened cocoa
  powder, sifted, for dusting

1 In a bowl, beat all the egg yolks and the sugar together until light and creamy using an electric hand mixer. Blend in the mascarpone and melted chocolate until combined.

2 In a separate bowl, whisk the egg whites until stiff but not dry. Using a metal spoon, fold the whisked whites into the mascarpone mixture.

3 In a clean bowl, combine the coffee and wine and dip the sponge-finger biscuits into the mixture, allowing them to soak up some of the liquid.

4 Use 10 of the soaked biscuits to line the base of a serving dish, around 28 x 18 x 6cm/11 x 7 x 2½in. Pour half the mascarpone mixture over the biscuits. Cover with the remaining biscuits, then the rest of the mascarpone. Dust with cocoa and sprinkle over the grated chocolate. Refrigerate for 2 hours.

EUROPE

Quickest-ever Dark Chocolate Mousse

PREPARATION TIME: 15 minutes, plus setting

FRANCE

SERVES 4

2 egg whites
5 tbsp caster (superfine) sugar
200g/7oz dark (bittersweet) chocolate, melted and left to cool
250ml/9fl oz/1 cup double (heavy) cream, whipped to soft peaks

1 In a large bowl, whisk the egg whites until soft peaks form using an electric hand mixer. Add the sugar gradually while continuing to whisk until the whites are thick and shiny. Using a metal spoon, fold in the melted chocolate and cream.

2 Using a large spoon, divide the mousse between 4 dishes, then refrigerate for 30 minutes before serving.

Mulled Berries with Chocolate Ice Cream

PREPARATION TIME: 20 minutes, plus cooling
COOKING TIME: 8 minutes

SERVES 4

280g/10oz/2 cups
  mixed berries
250ml/9fl oz/1 cup
  red wine
100g/3½oz/½ cup
  caster (granulated) sugar
grated zest and juice of
  1 orange
1 cinnamon stick
2 cloves
8 scoops Rich Chocolate
  Ice Cream (see page 30)
  or good-quality shop-
  bought ice cream

1 Place the berries in a bowl – slicing the strawberries and pitting the cherries, if using.

2 In a medium-size saucepan, heat the red wine, sugar, orange zest and juice, cinnamon stick and cloves until boiling. Lower the heat and simmer for 5 minutes, then remove from the heat. Leave to cool for 15 minutes, then pour the mulled wine mixture over the berries.

3 Place 2 scoops of ice cream in each of 4 tall glasses, then pour the warm berries over, along with some of the liquid. Serve immediately.

EUROPE

Coffee Liqueur Meringue with Chocolate

PREPARATION TIME: 30 minutes, plus cooling and chilling
COOKING TIME: 1 hour

IRELAND

MAKES: 1 x 23cm/ 9in meringue

6 egg whites
300g/10½oz/1½ cups caster (superfine) sugar
1 tbsp instant coffee granules, dissolved in ½ tsp warm water and cooled
1 tbsp unsweetened cocoa powder
375ml/13fl oz/1½ cups double (heavy) cream
2 tbsp coffee liqueur
100g/3½oz dark (bittersweet) chocolate, melted and cooled

1 Preheat the oven to 110°C/225°F/gas ¼. Line 2 baking trays with baking paper and draw 2 x 23cm/9in circles on the paper in pencil.

2 In a bowl, whisk the egg whites until stiff peaks form using an electric hand mixer, then gradually whisk in the sugar until the mixture is thick and shiny and the sugar has dissolved. Whisk in the coffee and cocoa. Spoon on to the trays and spread over the circles on the baking paper.

3 Bake in the warm oven for 1 hour until the meringue is crisp but not brown. Remove from the oven and leave the meringues to cool completely on the trays.

4 In a clean bowl, whip the cream and liqueur together using an electric hand mixer to form soft peaks. To assemble the meringue, place

EVERYBODY LOVES CHOCOLATE

1 meringue round on a serving plate, spread over half the liqueur cream and drizzle over half the melted chocolate. Place the second meringue round on top. Repeat with the remaining cream and chocolate for this top layer, then refrigerate for 2 hours before serving.

MIDDLE EAST & AFRICA

Israeli White Chocolate Cheesecake

PREPARATION TIME: 30 minutes, plus chilling

ISRAEL

MAKES: 1 x 23cm/9in
square cheesecake

250g/9oz plain sweet
  biscuits (cookies), crushed
  finely, plus 50g/1¾oz
  for the topping
120g/4¼oz/½ cup
  butter, melted
250g/9oz/1 cup cream
  cheese
200g/7oz/scant 1 cup
  crème fraîche
150g/5½oz white
  chocolate, melted
200g/7oz/¾ cup plus
  2 tbsp butter, softened
125g/4½oz/½ cup plus
  2 tbsp caster (granulated)
  sugar
1 tsp vanilla extract
1 egg, plus 1 yolk

1 Line a 23cm/9in square cake pan with overlapping rectangles of baking paper. This makes the cheesecake easy to remove. Mix the 250g/9oz crushed biscuits with the melted butter and evenly line the base of the cake pan, pressing down firmly. Refrigerate for 15 minutes.

2 Beat the cream cheese and crème fraîche in a bowl and fold in the melted white chocolate.

3 In a separate bowl, cream the butter, sugar and vanilla extract together until light, then add the egg and egg yolk. Beat again until the mixture is smooth. Gently fold the cream cheese mixture into the butter mixture.

4 Remove the cake pan from the refrigerator and pour over the cheesecake mixture, smoothing the top evenly. Sprinkle over the extra biscuit crumbs and refrigerate for 4 hours or overnight before serving. Cut into 16 squares to serve.

Chocolate-dipped Sesame & Honey Brittle

PREPARATION TIME: 25 minutes, plus cooling and setting
COOKING TIME: 8 minutes

MAKES: about 30 pieces

vegetable oil, for greasing
160g/5oz/⅔ cup caster
  (granulated) sugar
85g/3¾oz/¼ cup runny
  honey
pinch salt
150g/5½oz/1¼ cups
  untoasted sesame seeds
15g/½oz/1 tbsp butter,
  softened
1 tsp vanilla extract
¼ tsp bicarbonate of soda
  (baking soda)
100g/3½oz dark
  (bittersweet)
  chocolate, melted and
  cooled slightly

1 Grease a medium baking tray with vegetable oil.

2 Put the sugar, honey, salt and 1 tbsp water in a saucepan and heat over a low heat until the mixture is smooth. Add the sesame seeds and continue stirring until the mixture turns a light caramel colour. This will take around 5 minutes.

3 Remove the saucepan from the heat and add the butter and vanilla extract, stirring well. Then add the bicarbonate of soda – this will foam up slightly.

4 Working quickly, pour the sesame seed mixture on to the lightly oiled tray and spread thinly. Leave to cool completely before removing from the tray and breaking into bite-sized pieces with your hands.

5 Dip the brittle halfway into the melted chocolate, then leave to set on a wire (cooling) rack.

Chocolate Malva Pudding

PREPARATION TIME: 20 minutes
COOKING TIME: 25–30 minutes

SERVES 4–6

15g/½oz/1 tbsp butter,
    melted, plus extra for
    greasing
125g/4½oz/1 cup plain
    (all-purpose) flour
1 tbsp cocoa powder
1 tsp baking powder
180g/6¼oz/¾ cup plus
    2 tbsp caster (granulated)
    sugar
pinch salt
3 tbsp apricot jam
2 eggs, lightly beaten
1 tsp bicarbonate of soda
    (baking soda)
180ml/6fl oz/¾ cup milk
4 tsp white wine vinegar
1 recipe quantity Rich
    Chocolate Sauce
    (see page 25)

1 Preheat the oven to 180°C/350°F/gas 4.
Lightly grease a 20cm/8in square ovenproof
dish with butter.

2 Sift together the flour, cocoa and baking
powder in a bowl, then add the sugar and salt.
Stir together to combine.

3 In a large bowl, mix together the jam, eggs
and melted butter. Stir the bicarbonate of soda
into the milk, add the vinegar, then combine with
the jam, eggs and melted butter. Add to the dry
ingredients, mixing well to make a smooth batter.

4 Pour the mixture into the prepared dish and
bake for 25–30 minutes, or until the mixture is just
firm in the middle and a skewer comes out clean.
Serve with the rich chocolate sauce.

MIDDLE
EAST

Chocolate Cookies with Pistachios

PREPARATION TIME: 30 minutes, plus chilling and setting
COOKING TIME: 12 minutes

MAKES: 30 cookies

225g/8oz/scant 1 cup
   butter, softened
100g/3½oz/¾ cup
   icing (confectioners')
   sugar, sifted
1 tsp vanilla extract
2 eggs, lightly beaten
300g/10½oz/2¼ cups
   plain (all-purpose) flour,
   plus extra for dusting
1 tsp baking powder
1 tbsp unsweetened cocoa
   powder
70g/2½oz/¾ cup shelled
   pistachio nuts, to garnish

1 Cream the butter, sugar and vanilla together until light and fluffy using an electric hand mixer. Add the eggs, a little at a time, until well mixed.

2 Sift together the flour, baking powder and cocoa powder, then stir into the butter mixture, adding one-third at a time. When the mixture is well combined, place in the refrigerator for 20 minutes until slightly firm.

3 Preheat the oven to 180°C/350°F/gas 4. Line 2 large baking trays with baking paper.

4 Roll the dough into 30 small balls (around the size of a walnut) and place on the baking trays. Press each cookie lightly then gently press some of the chopped pistachios on top. Bake for 12 minutes, then leave to cool completely on the baking trays.

Turkish Chocolate & Caramel Pudding

PREPARATION TIME: 40 minutes, plus chilling
COOKING TIME: 40–50 minutes

SERVES 8–10

butter, for greasing
340ml 11¾fl oz/1⅓ cups
  evaporated milk
60ml/2fl oz/¼ cup
  condensed milk
100ml/3½fl oz/scant
  ½ cup double (heavy)
  cream
6 eggs
1 tsp vanilla extract
300g/10½oz/1½ cups
  caster (granulated) sugar
250g/9oz/1¾ cups plus
  2 tbsp plain (all-purpose)
  flour
1 tsp baking powder
1 tbsp unsweetened cocoa
  powder

1 Preheat the oven to 350°F/180°C/gas 4. Lightly grease an ovenproof dish, approximately 23 x 33cm/9 x 13in, with butter.

2 For the cake, place the evaporated milk, condensed milk and cream into a bowl and mix until well combined. Leave to one side.

3 Put the eggs in the bowl of a stand mixer with the vanilla extract and sugar and whisk until thick and creamy (around 4–5 minutes). Sift together the flour, baking powder and cocoa and gently fold into the egg mixture, one-third at a time.

4 Pour into the prepared dish and bake for 25–35 minutes until the mixture is firm in the middle and a skewer comes out clean. Leave to cool on a wire (cooling) rack for 5 minutes. Prick the cake all over with a skewer and carefully spoon half the milk

FOR THE CARAMEL SAUCE

250g/9oz/1¼ cups caster (granulated) sugar
200ml/7fl oz/scant 1 cup double (heavy) cream

FOR THE TOPPING

500ml/17fl oz/2 cups double (heavy) cream
25g/1oz/2 tbsp caster (granulated) sugar
1 tsp vanilla extract
grated dark (bittersweet) chocolate, to serve

mixture over the warm cake and leave to settle for a moment, then spoon over the remaining mixture. Be sure to cover the cake evenly. Leave for at least 1 hour to cool completely.

5 In the meantime, make the caramel sauce by placing the sugar and 125ml/4fl oz/½ cup water into a heavy saucepan over a low heat, stirring gently with a metal spoon until the sugar melts. Increase the heat and watch the mixture carefully, swirling the pan occasionally, until a dark golden caramel forms. Remove from the heat and add the cream. Return to a low heat, stirring, until the mixture is smooth. Remove from the heat, pour into a jug and leave to cool completely.

6 For the cream topping, whip the cream, sugar and vanilla extract together in a bowl until thick, taking care not to overwhip.

7 Spread a smooth, even layer of the cream over the cooled cake. Drizzle the caramel sauce over the cream and refrigerate for 1 hour until set. Decorate with grated chocolate to serve.

MIDDLE EAST

Chocolate, Sesame & Tahini Cookies

PREPARATION TIME: 15 minutes
COOKING TIME: 7–8 minutes

MAKES: 18 cookies

100g/3½oz/⅓ cup runny
  honey
75g/2¾oz/⅓ cup tahini
1 tsp vanilla extract
140g/5oz/1½ cups
  ground almonds
1 tbsp unsweetened cocoa
  powder, sifted
½ tsp baking powder
75g/2¾oz/heaped ½
  cup sesame seeds

1 Preheat the oven to 180°C/350°F/gas 4. Line a large baking tray with baking paper.

2 Mix together the honey, tahini and vanilla extract in a large bowl, then stir in the ground almonds, cocoa powder, baking powder and sesame seeds. Mix well.

3 Roll the mixture into 18 small balls with your hands, then place on the prepared baking tray. Flatten each cookie slightly with your hand.

4 Bake in the hot oven for 7–8 minutes until the cookies are slightly firm. Remove the cookies from the oven and transfer to a wire (cooling) rack to cool completely.

**MIDDLE
EAST**

Chocolate Fig Kindlech

PREPARATION TIME: 30 minutes, plus chilling
COOKING TIME: 20–25 minutes

MAKES: 24–32 pieces

240g/8½oz/1 cup plain
(all-purpose) flour, plus
extra for dusting
1 tbsp caster (granulated)
sugar, plus extra for dusting
125g/4½oz/½ cup butter,
chilled
2 egg yolks
75g/2¾oz/5 tbsp sour
cream
1 tsp vanilla extract
4 tbsp fig jam
125g/4½oz/¾ cup raisins
125g/4½oz dark
(bittersweet) chocolate,
roughly chopped
1 egg, beaten with
1 tsp water
2 tbsp toasted almonds,
to serve

1 Put the flour, sugar and butter in a food processor and pulse into breadcrumbs. Add the egg yolks, sour cream and vanilla extract and pulse until a dough forms. Be careful not to overwork this or the dough will become tough. Remove from the bowl and press together to form a disc, then wrap in cling film (plastic wrap) and chill in the refrigerator for 1 hour.

2 Preheat the oven to 180°C/350°F/gas 4. Line a large baking tray with baking paper.

3 Cut the dough into 4 pieces. On a lightly floured surface, roll out one piece of the dough to a thin rectangle measuring around 15 x 30cm/6 x 12in. Spread 1 tbsp of the jam over the dough and sprinkle ¼ of the raisins and chopped chocolate. Roll up the log, rolling from the short side. Place the roll on the prepared baking tray and brush lightly with the beaten egg mixture. Repeat with the remaining dough to make 3 more filled rolls.

4 Bake in the hot oven for 20–25 minutes until lightly browned. Remove from the oven and transfer to a wire (cooling) rack to cool completely. When cool, use a sharp knife to cut each roll widthways into 6–8 pieces. Sprinkle with a little caster sugar and toasted almonds to serve.

White Chocolate Mousse with Orange Blossom

PREPARATION TIME: 25 minutes, plus chilling
COOKING TIME: 5 minutes

SERVES 6

200g/7oz white
  chocolate, broken into
  pieces
2 egg whites
1 tbsp caster (superfine)
  sugar
300ml/10½fl oz/
  1¼ cups double
  (heavy) cream
2 tsp orange blossom
  water (to taste)
1 tbsp orange juice
2 tbsp grated orange zest

1 Melt the chocolate and leave to cool slightly. Place the egg whites in a large bowl and whisk until frothy using an electric hand mixer. Add the sugar and continue to whisk until the meringue is thick and shiny. Add the cooled chocolate and fold through gently.

2 Whip the cream with the orange blossom water, orange juice and 1 tbsp of the orange zest in a bowl until soft peaks just begin to form. Take care not to overmix.

3 Fold the whipped orange cream through the chocolate meringue mixture until combined. Spoon the mousse into 6 serving dishes and refrigerate for 30 minutes. Sprinkle with the remaining grated orange zest before serving.

Roast Figs with Chocolate Sauce

PREPARATION TIME: 10 minutes, plus cooling
COOKING TIME: 15–20 minutes

SERVES 4

75g/2¾oz/5 tbsp butter, plus extra for greasing
8 large figs
2 tbsp caster (granulated) sugar
4 tbsp double (heavy) cream, whipped to soft peaks
½ recipe quantity Rich Chocolate Sauce (see page 25)

1 Preheat the oven to 180°C/350°F/gas 4. Grease an ovenproof dish (large enough to hold the figs) with butter.

2 Cut a cross in the top of each fig, taking care to keep the fig in one piece. Divide the butter into 8 pieces and place one inside each fig. Place the figs in the prepared dish and sprinkle over the sugar.

3 Bake in the hot oven for 15–20 minutes, or until the figs are soft but still hold their shape. Remove from the oven and set the baked figs aside in the dish to cool for 10 minutes.

4 Divide the figs between 4 plates, top with a spoonful of cream and pour over the rich chocolate sauce.

MIDDLE EAST

Chocolate, Ginger & Tahini Fruit & Nut Squares

PREPARATION TIME: 20 minutes, plus chilling
COOKING TIME: 15 minutes

MIDDLE EAST

MAKES: 30 squares

200g/7oz ginger biscuits (cookies), lightly crushed
75g/2¾oz/½ cup shelled pistachio nuts, roughly chopped
75g/2¾oz/½ cup raisins
30g/1oz/¼ cup pumpkin seeds
30g/1oz/¼ cup sesame seeds
200g/7oz dark (bittersweet) chocolate, broken into pieces
2 tbsp tahini

1 Line a 20cm/8in square cake pan with baking paper. Place the lightly crushed biscuits (reserving 2 tbsp to decorate), pistachios, raisins and pumpkin and sesame seeds in a bowl.

2 Melt the chocolate and tahini together in a heatproof bowl set over a pan of simmering water and stir until smooth. Pour over the biscuit mixture and stir to fully coat the dry ingredients.

3 Spoon the mixture into the prepared pan and smooth the top. Sprinkle over the reserved crushed biscuits and smooth the top. Chill in the refrigerator for around 2 hours before cutting into 30 squares.

MIDDLE EAST

Chocolate Rum Truffles

PREPARATION TIME: 20 minutes, plus cooling and chilling
COOKING TIME: 5 minutes

IRAQ

MAKES: 18 truffles

150g/5½oz dark
   (bittersweet) chocolate,
   broken into pieces
4 tbsp double (heavy)
   cream
3 tbsp rum
200g/7oz/1 cup
   chocolate sprinkles

1 In a small saucepan, combine the chocolate and cream over a low heat until the chocolate has just melted, stirring frequently with a wooden spoon. Remove from the heat and stir in the rum. Pour into a heatproof bowl and leave to cool completely, then refrigerate for approximately 30 minutes until firm.

2 Roll teaspoonfuls of the mixture into balls and toss in the chocolate sprinkles to coat. Place on a baking tray lined with baking paper and refrigerate for 1 hour until firm.

Chocolate-dipped Dried Fruits

PREPARATION TIME: 15 minutes, plus chilling
COOKING TIME: 5 minutes

MIDDLE EAST

MAKES: 24 chocolates

250g/9oz dark
(bittersweet) chocolate,
broken into pieces
24 pieces dried fruit,
including apricots,
pear and pineapple

1 In a small saucepan, heat the chocolate over a low heat until just melted, then remove from the heat and stir until smooth.

2 Wipe the dried fruit with paper towels, then dip each piece in the melted chocolate to cover halfway. (If the chocolate runs off without making a nice coating, leave it to cool for a few minutes, then try again.)

3 Place the dipped fruit on a baking tray lined with baking paper and refrigerate for around 30 minutes until the chocolate has set.

Candied Citrus Peel

PREPARATION TIME: 25 minutes, plus cooling and setting
COOKING TIME: 25 minutes

MIDDLE EAST

MAKES: 24 pieces

3 lemons or oranges
5 tbsp granulated sugar
100g/3½oz dark
   (bittersweet) chocolate,
   melted and left to cool

1 Remove the peel from the fruit using a wide-bladed vegetable peeler. Using a sharp knife, cut away any remaining white pith and cut the rind into strips around 1cm/½in wide. Place the strips in a saucepan, cover with water and bring to the boil. Drain immediately in a colander, then refresh under cold water.

2 In a small saucepan, heat the sugar and 125ml/4fl oz/½ cup water over a medium heat until the sugar has dissolved, then add the blanched rind. Continue to cook over a medium heat for around 15 minutes until the liquid is syrupy and the peel is bright-coloured and shiny. Remove the peel from the water using a slotted spoon and place on baking paper to cool.

3 Half-dip each piece of candied citrus peel in the chocolate and leave on baking paper to set.

MIDDLE
EAST

Marzipan-stuffed Chocolate Dates

PREPARATION TIME: 20 minutes, plus setting

MIDDLE EAST

MAKES: 20 chocolate dates

75g/2¾oz marzipan
20 large dates, split in half
  and pits removed
150g/5½oz dark
  (bittersweet) chocolate,
  melted and left to cool

1 Knead the marzipan until soft, then roll into 20 small oblong shapes to fit inside each of the dates.

2 Either dip each date into the melted chocolate to coat half or line up the dates on a baking tray lined and drizzle the chocolate over the top of them. Leave at room temperature to set, then place in petit four cases to serve.

MIDDLE
EAST

Chocolate Nougat Ice Cream

PREPARATION TIME: 20 minutes, plus chilling and churning
COOKING TIME: 5 minutes

MAKES: 1l/35fl oz/
4¼ cups

300ml/10½fl oz/
    1¼ cups milk
200g/7oz dark
    (bittersweet) chocolate,
    broken into pieces
4 egg yolks
100g/3½oz/½ cup
    caster (granulated) sugar
300ml/10½fl oz/1¼
    cups double (heavy)
    cream
100g/3½oz soft nougat,
    finely chopped
1 tsp vanilla extract

1 In a small saucepan, heat the milk and chocolate together over a low heat until the chocolate has just melted.

2 In a large bowl, beat the egg yolks and sugar together using a hand whisk, then whisk in the warm chocolate milk. Return the mixture to the pan and heat, stirring constantly with a wooden spoon, until the mixture just begins to thicken and lightly coats the back of the spoon. Do not allow the mixture to boil, as it will curdle.

3 Remove from the heat, pour into a heatproof bowl, cover with cling film (plastic wrap) and leave to cool completely. Refrigerate for 3 hours or overnight.

4 Remove from the refrigerator and stir in the cream, nougat and vanilla extract, then churn in an ice-cream machine according to the manufacturer's instructions.

Turkish Delight Ice Cream

PREPARATION TIME: 20 minutes, plus chilling and churning
COOKING TIME: 5 minutes

MAKES: 1l/35fl oz/
4¼ cups

300ml/10½fl oz/
   1¼ cups milk
500ml/17fl oz/2 cups
   double (heavy) cream
200g/7oz dark
   (bittersweet) chocolate,
   broken into pieces
100g/3½oz/½ cup
   caster (granulated) sugar
4 egg yolks
200g/7oz Turkish delight
   (any variety), chopped
1 tbsp rosewater (optional)

1 In a medium-size saucepan, heat the milk, cream and chocolate together over a low heat until the chocolate has just melted.

2 In a large, heatproof bowl, beat the sugar and egg yolks together using a hand whisk, then pour in the chocolate mixture, whisking constantly. Return the mixture to the pan and heat, stirring constantly with a wooden spoon, until the mixture just begins to thicken and lightly coats the back of the spoon. Do not let it boil, as it will curdle.

3 Remove from the heat, pour into a clean, heatproof bowl and leave to cool completely. Refrigerate for 3 hours or overnight.

4 Stir in the chopped Turkish delight and rosewater, if using, then churn in an ice-cream machine according to the manufacturer's instructions.

MIDDLE
EAST

White Chocolate Rice Pudding with Rosewater & Pomegranate

PREPARATION TIME: 15 minutes
COOKING TIME: 30–35 minutes

SERVES 6

500ml/17fl oz/2
  cups milk
200ml/7fl oz/scant 1 cup
  double (heavy) cream
150g/5½oz/⅔ cup
  short-grain rice
1 tbsp caster (granulated)
  sugar
100g/3½oz white
  chocolate, broken into
  small pieces
1 tsp rosewater (to taste)
3 tbsp pomegranate seeds
75g/2¾oz/½ cup shelled
  roasted pistachio nuts,
  roughly chopped (optional)

1 Place the milk and cream in a large saucepan over a low heat and bring to the boil.

2 Rinse the rice well under cold water and add to the milk mixture along with the sugar. Return to the boil, stirring well, then reduce to a low simmer for 25–30 minutes, or until the rice is tender, stirring often to prevent it from sticking.

3 Stir in the chocolate until it melts. Serve warm or at room temperature. Before serving, stir in the rosewater to taste and sprinkle with the pomegranate seeds and, if using, the roasted pistachios.

ABOUT THE AUTHOR

Jennifer Donovan was born in Australia where she trained and developed her passion for good food. After many years in London she is now based in the Gloucestershire countryside, where she writes and continues to develop new recipes. She is the author of *The Easy Italian Cookbook*.

ACKNOWLEDGEMENTS

My sincerest thanks go to the wonderful team at Watkins for all of their hard work in putting this book together. It has truly been a group effort. My particular thanks goes to the Designer, Sneha Alexander, and the Project Editor, Brittany Willis, whose incredible talent has produced such a beautiful book.

INDEX

INDEX

/ERYBODY LOVES CHOCOLATE